AF575155

FAULKNER'S FABLES OF CREATIVITY

Faulkner's Fables of Creativity

The Non-Yoknapatawpha Novels

Gary Harrington

The University of Georgia Press
Athens

Published in the United States of America in 1990 by
The University of Georgia Press, Athens, Georgia 30602

First published in Great Britain in 1990 by Macmillan

Printed in Hong Kong

Library of Congress Cataloging in Publication Data
Harrington, Gary.
Faulkner's fables of creativity: The non-Yoknapatawpha novels/Gary Harrington.
p. cm.
Bibliography: p.
Includes index.
ISBN 0–8203–1098–0
1. Faulkner, William, 1897–1967—Criticism and interpretation.
2. Creativity in literature. 3. Artists in literature. I. Title.
PS3511.A86Z78456 1990
813'.52—dc19 88–17309
CIP

To my father, Daniel, and my mother, Marie

Contents

Preface

The two principal turning-points in Faulkner's early career consisted in his abandonment of poetry in favor of prose fiction and his embarkation upon the process of exploring his mythical county of Yoknapatawpha—an undertaking which was to consume the greater part of his writing life. At once separating and linking the two vocational climacterics were Faulkner's first two novels, *Soldiers' Pay* and *Mosquitoes*, the lessons he learned while composing these overtly experimental texts and the dissatisfactions he felt with the results having jointly compelled his crucial recognition of the extraordinary potential for fictional development latent in his own 'little postage stamp of native soil'. This commitment to Yoknapatawpha did not, however, prevent Faulkner from purposively choosing areas beyond the borders as the primary settings for three of his later novels, *Pylon, The Wild Palms*, and *A Fable*, chiefly (as I shall argue) as a means of conducting indirect investigations of the responsibilities attendant upon his vocation as a novelist and of probing into the myriad complexities inherent in the relationships among writers, readers and texts.

Since the first two novels, as the work of a fledgling writer seeking his own authorial voice, had necessarily reflected the same or very similar concerns, the five non-Yoknapatawpha novels can be seen as constituting what I have called 'fables of creativity'—a series of profound if sometimes unresolved Faulknerian reflections on aesthetic and creative issues. As such, these texts deserve a much closer and more comprehensive scrutiny than they have thus far received—one capable of yielding insights not only into the works themselves but into Faulkner's deliberate yet flexible shaping of his canon, his responses to contemporary literary trends, his imaginative processes, and his attitudes towards his vocation and his audience. Ultimately, as I shall attempt to show, it is precisely by virtue of their apparent idiosyncrasy and eccentricity within the Faulkner canon that the non-Yoknapatawpha novels can enhance our understanding both of the mainstream Yoknapatawpha works and of the shape and content of Faulkner's career as a whole.

I am grateful to Professors Ruth and Lawrence Miller for reading and commenting upon the early stages of this book, and to the Department of Humanities and Social Sciences at the Montana College of Mineral Science and Technology for providing the reduction in my teaching load which enabled me to complete the final revisions. Professor Thomas L. McHaney's remarks upon an early version of the text were most helpful, and his book *William Faulkner's 'The Wild Palms': A Study* fully attests to the value of giving the non-Yoknapatawphan Faulkner serious and sympathetic attention. I would like to extend my thanks to the *Dalhousie Review* and *The Faulkner Journal* for permission to republish in a slightly different form material which first appeared in those journals. The publication of this book owes much to Ms Evelyn Tracy, whose word-processing wizardry is surpassed only by her remarkable patience and consistent good humor. The Salisbury State University Foundation generously provided financial support which expedited the preparation of this book's later stages, and Ms. Lori Beste supplied diligent and meticulous assistance in that preparation. It gives me particular pleasure to acknowledge here a signal debt of gratitude to Professor Michael Millgate, whose unstinting generosity with his time, knowledge, and encouragement contributed immensely to the realization of this text. Finally, I would like to thank the members of my family—and particularly my parents—for their unflagging affection and support.

GARY HARRINGTON

1
Introduction

The very designation 'non-Yoknapatawpha' serves to suggest the anomalous position which *Soldiers' Pay, Mosquitoes, Pylon, The Wild Palms,* and *A Fable* occupy within the Faulkner canon. That these novels as a group are customarily defined in terms of what they are *not* attests to the overwhelming power which the Yoknapatawpha texts exert on the general estimation of Faulkner's career. In some respects, this response seems appropriate since there can be no question that Yoknapatawpha constitutes the heart of the canon. Nevertheless, 'non-Yoknapatawpha' must be construed as a rather misleading term if it is taken to imply that these novels are intrinsically less important than—and entirely unrelated to—those novels set in Faulkner's fictional county.

Partly because a satisfactory definition of Yoknapatawpha itself has yet to be offered, any examination of the non-Yoknapatawpha novels as a group must at the present time be largely tentative and exploratory. Furthermore, little scholarly attention has as yet been devoted to them, apparently a reflection of the widely held opinion that they remain superfluous or at any rate non-essential to the canon. Some fine analyses of the individual novels have certainly appeared, and these may ultimately help to counteract that view: Margaret Yonce's dissertation and her articles on *Soldiers' Pay*, Thomas L. McHaney's *William Faulkner's 'The Wild Palms': A Study*, and Keen Butterworth's analysis of *A Fable*—all have enhanced our understanding of individual non-Yoknapatawpha novels in isolation one from another.[1] Even so, at present the general neglect of the novels individually and collectively continues.

Of the few studies devoted to the non-Yoknapatawpha novels as a group that have thus far appeared, the most notable is, of course, Cleanth Brooks's *William Faulkner: Toward Yoknapatawpha and Beyond*.[2] Brooks's analyses, while often stimulating, nonetheless remain somewhat limited; as McHaney has observed, that idealized interpretation of community informing Brooks's earlier

William Faulkner: The Yoknapatawpha Country serves to render the non-Yoknapatawpha novels as discussed in *Toward Yoknapatawpha and Beyond* deficient solely because of their exclusion from Yoknapatawpha.[3] Jefferson, however, hardly represented for Faulkner an ideal refuge from the vicissitudes of modern life, and to fault the non-Yoknapatawpha novels merely for being set outside of the fictional county seems a less than fruitful—or fair—approach. *Toward Yoknapatawpha and Beyond* includes chapters on the poetry and early prose, as well as a series of appendices, some of which—such as that on *Absalom, Absalom!*—have little direct bearing on the non-Yoknapatawpha works. The resulting diffusion of perspective prevents the interpretations of the individual novels from coalescing into an exploration of their function as a group within the canon as a whole.

Most of the relatively scant commentary devoted to the non-Yoknapatawpha fiction adopts just such an approach, implicitly assuming that although these five novels may have some marginal value as individual works they bear little relation to each other or to the canon. Yet such an approach runs contrary to Faulkner's assertions that the writer's total output should have a 'design'.[4] Although Faulkner's retrospective assessments of the shape of his literary career relate most directly to the myriad and intricate relationships among the Yoknapatawpha works, Faulkner himself did not exclude the non-Yoknapatawpha novels and there is no reason for the Faulkner scholar to ostracize them either. Indeed, the very fact that Faulkner chose to depart from the apparently inexhaustible resources of his fictional county and light out for unexplored fictional territories—at least insofar as the last three non-Yoknapatawpha novels are concerned—constitutes one of the most intriguing questions with which Faulkner scholarship must contend.

Although Faulkner's Yoknapatawpha characters may travel beyond the county limits, he never allows a direct reference to Yoknapatawpha to intrude upon the non-Yoknapatawpha works, and the extent to which he deliberately divorces *Pylon, The Wild Palms* and *A Fable* from Yoknapatawpha, even when skirting its borders (as in 'Old Man' and in the horsethief episode in *A Fable*), provides some clues concerning his purpose in writing them. The non-Yoknapatawpha novels may thus be seen to reflect Faulkner's perception of art as embodying universals, as treating the eternal verities of the human condition within the context of the variables of time and circumstance: what holds true in Yoknapatawpha, Faulkner's 'cosmos', remains equally valid in the world at large, and vice versa. In fact, Faulkner's most overtly philosophical and abstract treatment of the ubiquitous and eternal nature of the verities of human experience occurs in *A Fable*, the main setting of which is the farthest removed from Yoknapatawpha of any in his fiction.

The dissociation of *Pylon*, *The Wild Palms* and *A Fable* from Yoknapatawpha may also reflect a desire on Faulkner's part to demonstrate, particularly in the aggressively modernist thirties, that he was no local-colorist but could tackle other kinds of novels as effectively as any of his contemporaries. *Pylon*, *The Wild Palms* and, in a less direct way, *A Fable* respond in part to contemporary trends in fiction and so demonstrate Faulkner's capacity to stamp with his unmistakable imprint work which might not have been regarded as entirely congenial to his talents or his inclinations.

At the times when *Pylon* and *The Wild Palms* were published, and even while *A Fable* was being composed, the contemporary reception of Faulkner's work exhibited a profound lack of sympathy and understanding. That these three novels remain distinctively Faulknerian without being Yoknapatawphan may therefore indicate that Faulkner was using them in part to recommend a reassessment not only of his abilities as a writer but also of the canon as it had developed to that point, perhaps obliquely suggesting that the reader might use these experiments in literary contemporaneity as the basis for just such a reassessment—in effect, as fictive primers to the interpretation of the canon. *Pylon*'s explorations of the multivalence of truth and the centrality of the interpreting consciousness, for example, re-emerge as two of the primary concerns of *Absalom, Absalom!*—the novel whose composition Faulkner interrupted to write *Pylon*—and they figure prominently in many of his earlier and later novels as well. The radical juxtaposition of 'Wild Palms' and 'Old Man' in *The Wild Palms* exhibits the typical Faulknerian devices of opposition and suspension so prominent in such central Faulkner texts as the earlier *The Sound and the Fury* and the later *Go Down, Moses*. Indeed, with its two settings tangential to, but not intersecting, one another, *The Wild Palms* may even be read as in some sense representative of the complex relationships among the non-Yoknapatawpha and the Yoknapatawpha works. And the very title of *A Fable*, the work which Faulkner intended to be his *magnum opus*, underscores the fabular aspects of his literary output in general, the subtly interconnected fables in the novel suggesting a variety of approaches to the canon itself and intimating that Faulkner considered all of his fiction to be essentially one work, a single author's attempt to formulate and encompass the myth of the human condition.

This use of the non-Yoknapatawpha novels as a means of access to an understanding of the canon itself entails, almost of necessity, an exploration into the responsibilities of the reader—a circumstance which in its turn provides some justification for considering *Soldiers' Pay* and *Mosquitoes* as non-Yoknapatawphan as well as pre-Yoknapatawphan texts.[5] Gilligan, Jones, Donald, and the Rector in *Soldiers' Pay*, most of the major characters in *Mosquitoes*, the reporter in *Pylon*, Harry, Charlotte, and the tall convict in *The Wild Palms*, and Levine, the Norman, the runner, and the priest in *A Fable*—all are readers, and most evince a remarkable lack of perspicacity in their reading. Insofar as these characters' defects as readers correspond to their inadequate and usually polarized attitudes towards life, each of the non-Yoknapatawpha novels can be seen as presenting a cautionary fable which implies a necessary correlation between appropriate responses to literature and legitimate approaches to life.

The plethora of artist-figures in the non-Yoknapatawpha fiction indicates that Faulkner further uses these novels to endorse, primarily through a series of negative examples, a positive formulation of the role of the artist. Most of the readers within the non-Yoknapatawpha novels are also fabulists in that they construct elaborate fictions through which they attempt to come to terms with the world, to interpret and circumscribe the meaning of events and to define their own positions in light of those interpretations. They generally fail in their attempts, largely because of their refusal to accept that typically Faulknerian view of truth as encompassing two or more opposed yet at least partially valid perspectives. The reporter in *Pylon*, for example, characterizes the fliers at one time as non-human, at the next as superhuman, remaining adamant in his refusal to see the fliers as simply human. The reporter's own spectral appearance emerges in the course of the novel as emblematic of his inability to 'humanize' those whom he enlists as characters within his own personal drama.

Such extremes of attitude become prominent in each of the non-Yoknapatawphan works. Fanatics of one sort or another appear in abundance: Gordon, the reporter, Charlotte, the tall convict, and most of the principal characters in *A Fable*—all conceive of themselves as fulfilling a mission of some kind and exhibit a willingness to employ any means to accomplish their ends. The fact that most of these characters are also failed artist-figures serves to indicate Faulkner's recognition that fanaticism leads to proselytization rather than to art, and ultimately to destruction rather than to creation. Yoknapatawpha, of course, has its own share of fanatics—Doc Hines, Percy Grimm, Thomas Sutpen, Nancy Mannigoe, and even, in his own subterranean fashion, Flem Snopes—but most rest easy with their extremist views and never deviate from their respective designs. Their non-Yoknapatawpha counterparts, on the other hand, tend to be insecure in their creeds, and their strident disavowal of the possibility of perspectives differing from their own presents merely another manifestation of the way in which they flee, often literally, from the recognition of such a possibility.

The non-Yoknapatawpha characters in general also display intense forms of alienation, feeling disoriented and displaced in whatever location or situation they find themselves. While Faulkner never presents Jefferson as an ideal community—never allows it, for example, to assume that status as a haven from the loud world which Parchman represents for the tall convict—the sense of place is nevertheless crucial to the Yoknapatawpha fiction. One reason why Faulkner refused to permit any direct allusion to his fictional county in the non-Yoknapatawpha fiction may have been precisely that he wished to emphasise the deracination of so many of the non-Yoknapatawpha characters. In *Pylon*, Laverne's poignant plea for a home captures the plight of the fliers and mirrors the displacement and alienation of the reporter himself, who looks so utterly non-human that Hagood, the editor of the newspaper for which the reporter works, expresses amazement upon discovering that the reporter actually has a mother. Charlotte and Harry in *The Wild Palms* believe that their peregrinations provide an escape from the conventionality of hearth and home, but many of their problems—including Charlotte's unwanted pregnancy and, consequently, the botched abortion—stem in fact from their lack of a stable living situation. And there are so many orphans in *A Fable* that it seems almost as if Faulkner were starting a literary adoption agency. Even in the two novels written prior to Faulkner's discovery of his 'little postage stamp of native soil', uprootedness and spiritual orphanage play a pronounced role:

Gilligan apparently has no fixed destination on the train trip which opens *Soldiers' Pay,* Margaret Powers has no family ties and eventually travels to Atlanta with no definite objective in mind, and Donald Mahon—the soldier returning to his hometown—recognizes neither the town nor his family and friends. The artists and others aboard the yacht in *Mosquitoes* are both literally and metaphorically 'at sea', their total inability to adapt to the unfamiliar environment being epitomized by their ludicrous efforts to free the *Nausikaa* from the sand-bar on which it has run aground.

The heavily autobiographical content of *Soldiers' Pay* and *Mosquitoes* also aligns them with the later non-Yoknapatawpha works. Lowe and Jones in *Soldiers' Pay* display a number of the young Faulkner's characteristic attitudes and mannerisms, as do Gordon, Talliaferro and, of course, the character named Faulkner in *Mosquitoes*. Indeed, the setting and much of the basic plot for *Mosquitoes* derive from Faulkner's own experiences on an outing which took place while he was living in New Orleans.[6] While one perhaps expects an author's early work to be comprised largely of autobiographical material, it seems surprising that the later non-Yoknapatawpha works should contain so many autobiographical elements and references. Of course, Faulkner's personal experience in one way or another provides the basis for much of his fiction; in the non-Yoknapatawpha novels, however, personal references tend to be not only more extensive than elsewhere but more dramatic in that they occur in material which Faulkner deliberately divorced from Oxford, from Jefferson, and from the central portion of his canon. *Pylon* is partially based on events and people associated with the opening of Shushan Airport in New Orleans which Faulkner attended in 1934;[7] both Harry Wilbourne and the tall convict in *The Wild Palms* have experiences relating to Faulkner's own, while Charlotte is in many respects an amalgamation of Helen Baird and Meta Carpenter; and even in *A Fable,* where many of the characters come to be embodiments of opposed philosophical positions, the presentation of Levine resonates with correspondences to Faulkner's much earlier portrayal of Lowe's—and therefore, at least in part, of his own—attitudes and experiences.

A more central aspect of *A Fable* involves the extent to which the generalissimo and the Corporal can be read as representing opposing tendencies in the artist: the need, on the one hand, to cling to the earth to garner material and, on the other, the artistic imperative to allow the imagination free rein in order to invest this material with the status of myth. A related conflict appears in *The Wild Palms*, in which Charlotte's desire for rampant freedom serves as a corollary to the artist's desire for untrammeled expression, while the tall convict's insistence on order reflects the necessity of arranging that expression within some sort of structure. The reporter's flawed narration in *Pylon* seems almost to present a casebook study of how *not* to treat one's characters: he swings between sympathizing with the fliers to such an extent that he identifies totally with them and putting himself at such a remove that he imagines them to be of a different species than himself. The anonymity of the reporter, of the tall convict, and of so many of the characters in *A Fable* seems designed to project them as everyman or, perhaps more appropriately, 'every artist' figures—although in the non-Yoknapatawpha novels the sheer numbers of artist-figures cause such a distinction to become blurred. The most sustained of Faulkner's early explorations of the sources, function and meaning of art takes place in *Mosquitoes*, and the discussions aboard the yacht, although apparently flippant, do in fact revolve around concerns crucial to Faulkner himself as he embarked upon his literary career. In *Soldiers' Pay*, Faulkner treats specifically artistic concerns with less sophistication than in the later novels, but the oppositions among the uses to which Gilligan, Jones and the Rector put their reading present, in seminal form, one of those implicit comparisons of the merits of diverse perspectives on art which Faulkner was to develop much more elaborately in the succeeding non-Yoknapatawpha fiction.

In particular, the wide variety of literary allusions in *Soldiers' Pay* indicates the centrality of literature and language to the thematic concerns of the work and sets a precedent which was to be followed in each of the later non-Yoknapatawpha novels. In *Soldiers' Pay* and, to a lesser extent, in *Mosquitoes*, Faulkner may have been in part indulging a young author's vanity with regard to his reading. In the later non-Yoknapatawpha novels, he handles the allusions more adroitly and integrates them more fully. They also appear with a greater frequency and a greater prominence than in the Yoknapatawpha fiction. To some extent, these allusions may have been intended as a corrective to the contemporary conception of Faulkner as an unlearned bumpkin who, mud between his toes, sat in the barnyard and churned out Yoknapatawpha stories which deliberately—and perversely—eluded comprehension. More importantly, the abundantly allusive texture of the non-Yoknapatawpha fiction both implies a standard against which Faulkner's own work might be judged and illustrates his sense of continuity—of consanguinity, so to speak—with previous literary figures. Although contemporary public and critical opinion may have expressed reservations about Faulkner's merits as a writer, he entertained no such doubts himself, and the myriad allusions in the non-Yoknapatawpha fiction testify to his confidence that he would one day assume his rightful place as one of the masters of world literature.

They also illustrate the extent to which Faulkner quite self-consciously devoted the non-Yoknapatawpha works to explorations of the relationships between art and artist and between artist and reader—explorations which demonstrably influenced the development of the canon as a whole. Faulkner's emphasis on the symbiotic nature of the relationship between writer and reader, every reading consisting of a joint enterprise between the two, should come as no surprise to anyone familiar with Faulkner's notoriously difficult—and immensely rewarding—works. What may be more surprising is that the five novels which have been for so long largely ignored by Faulkner scholars should contain, if not a single key to the canon, then certainly an abundance of hints and clues as to the way in which all of Faulkner's works should individually and collectively be read. The succeeding chapters argue that the non-Yoknapatawpha novels as a group constitute Faulkner's most intensive investigation into the tribulations, rewards, and responsibilities of his vocation with regard to both artist and audience—that they are, in essence, fables of creativity.

2

Soldiers' Pay

During the formative period in 1925 when Faulkner was residing in New Orleans, his friend Phil Stone in Oxford became concerned at not having heard from him for some time and sent him a wire: 'WHATS THE MATTER? DO YOU HAVE A MISTRESS?' Faulkner replied by telegram: 'YES. AND SHES 30,000 WORDS LONG'.[1] The 'mistress' in this exchange eventually developed into Faulkner's first novel, *Soldiers' Pay*. He apparently started work on the book, originally entitled 'Mayday',[2] in the early months of 1925 and, with the exception of a brief visit to Oxford in late February, remained in New Orleans until completion of the final draft in May. That same summer it was submitted to Liveright, Sherwood Anderson's publisher, who, largely on Anderson's recommendation, accepted it, changed the title, and published it as *Soldiers' Pay* on 25 February 1926.[3]

The reviews which followed shortly thereafter were generally positive: although a number noted the 'purple prose' passages in the work, many nonetheless considered it to be a fine novel and a favorable portent of Faulkner's future as a novelist.[4] *Soldiers' Pay* did not sell particularly well, however, and it later shared in that general disregard of all of Faulkner's works which persisted into the late forties and early fifties; indeed, even after the Faulkner canon had begun to be more thoroughly investigated, *Soldiers' Pay*—as an early work set in a place called Charlestown, Georgia, which does not recur in any of Faulkner's later novels or stories—tended to be relegated to the background while attention was focused on the Yoknapatawpha fiction. This situation has not greatly changed at present, even though essays by Olga Vickery, Michael Millgate, Cleanth Brooks, and Margaret Yonce have greatly enhanced our understanding of the novel.[5] *Soldiers' Pay*, like *Mosquitoes*, is still generally considered solely in terms of its position in Faulkner's 'apprenticeship' period, studies of the novel concentrating primarily upon the manner in which Faulkner transported or altered techniques and idiosyncrasies in style, themes, characterization and structure in the process of moving from his early work to the Yoknapatawpha mainstream.

It must be said, of course, that an approach which centers on the relation of *Soldiers' Pay* to the canon as a whole does yield substantial results. For example, the repetition of key descriptive phrases in this first novel anticipates the way in which Faulkner was later to incorporate essentially poetic means of expression into his mature fiction, and often represents an attempt to indicate that simultaneity of action which was to become such an important factor in his later work. The use of elevated language to express a level of emotion which the character would be incapable of verbalizing—as in the description of George Farr's feelings about Cecily Saunders while she is at the dance[6]—relates to Faulkner's later use of the same technique in, for instance, *As I Lay Dying, The Hamlet*, and *The Mansion*. A self-imposed sterility like that of the Reverend Mahon, often played off against a background of natural fecundity, is crucial to the presentation of many Yoknapatawphan figures—in this respect the Rector resembles, for example, Gail Hightower of *Light in August* and Ike McCaslin of *Go Down, Moses*. Other characters in *Soldiers' Pay* also have successors in subsequent Faulkner novels: Emmy appears to be an early conception of the earth-mother figure later embodied by Lena Grove and Eula Varner; Julian Lowe anticipates a variety of other Faulkner characters, most notably Levine in *A Fable*; and Cecily shares some features with Patricia Robyn in *Mosquitoes* and Temple Drake in *Sanctuary*. Most importantly, perhaps, the yoking together of heterogeneous blocks of material in *Soldiers' Pay* establishes a precedent upon which Faulkner was to play variations throughout his career.

It could well be that the juxtaposition of seemingly disparate blocks of material in *Soldiers' Pay* was suggested to Faulkner by his reading of Sherwood Anderson's *Winesburg, Ohio*. In an article which Faulkner wrote in 1925 evaluating Anderson's work, he singled out *Winesburg* as the finest of Anderson's literary accomplishments,[7] a judgment reflected in a prominent allusion to *Winesburg* in *Soldiers' Pay*. In Faulkner's novel, as the Rector and Gilligan walk through the countryside on the way to their potentially epiphanic moment outside the shabby church, they pass 'a small house, sleeping among climbing roses' (318). Beyond the house 'an orchard slept the night away in symmetrical rows, squatting and pregnant', and the Rector observes, 'Willard has good fruit' (318). It seems likely that the name 'Willard' alludes to George Willard, the central character in *Winesburg*. Given the 'wasteland' ambience of so much of *Soldiers' Pay*, the association of the *Winesburg* allusion with the 'pregnant' orchard teeming with life and the 'pure quivering chord of music' (318) issuing from the church emphasises the potential of an imagination rooted in the earth to achieve some type of spiritual regeneration. Faulkner's description in his 1925 essay of Anderson's talents as a writer anticipates in its linking of natural fertility and literary productivity that context in which the allusion to *Winesburg* was later to be placed in *Soldiers' Pay*:

> Men grow from the soil, like corn and trees: I prefer to think of Mr. Anderson as a lusty corn field in his native Ohio. . . . And behind all of [the characters in *Winesburg* is] a ground of fecund earth and corn in the green spring and the slow, full hot summer and the rigorous masculine winter that hurts it not, but makes it stronger.[8]

Although Faulkner's own 'little postage stamp of native soil' was ultimately to prove immeasurably richer than Anderson's, the reference to the fecundity of Willard's orchard in *Soldiers' Pay* demonstrates Faulkner's early awareness and appreciation of the seed planted in his own fertile imagination by Anderson both as man and as artist. Anderson's *Dark Laughter* also may have influenced some of the detail in Faulkner's novel: the references in *Dark Laughter* to the manner in which black singing and laughter have 'a way of getting at the ultimate truth of things'[9] resonate in the conclusion of *Soldiers' Pay* and Sponge Martin's attitude towards his daughter after discovering her *in flagrante delicto* resembles that of Emmy's father after he becomes aware of her liaison with Donald.

Dark Laughter, for its part, owes a debt to Joyce's *Ulysses*, which is specifically mentioned in Anderson's novel, and it appears that in *Soldiers' Pay* Faulkner was drawing, directly or indirectly, on the same source. Whether Faulkner had read *Ulysses*, in part or in its entirety, prior to beginning work on *Soldiers' Pay* is a vexed and vexing question and one which may well remain unanswered. Even if he had not read *Ulysses* as a whole, however, he had probably gleaned enough from extracts or from conversations with those who had read it to be familiar with the book's general contours. Textual evidence in *Soldiers' Pay* indicates at least a passing acquaintance with *Ulysses*: the interior monologues, although conceivably suggested by *A Portrait of the Artist as a Young Man*, correspond more closely in tone and manner to those in *Ulysses*, while the section of *Soldiers' Pay* entitled 'Voices' resembles in some ways Joyce's 'Sirens' and 'Circe' episodes. Nevertheless, several aspects of *Soldiers' Pay*—including the enclosure in parentheses of most of the interior monologues and the juxtaposition in the 'Voices' section of the collective voice of Charlestown with fragments of internal monologue and straight dialogue—indicate that even while adopting certain Joycean narrative techniques Faulkner was altering or expanding them to suit his own objectives.

Januarius Jones, plump if not stately, seems in many respects to be a kind of backwater Buck Mulligan: like Buck, he is irreverent, familiar with classical languages, well-read, and somewhat sinister despite his humorous demeanor. Jones nonetheless stands independently as a figure in his own right, his distinctive characteristics including his desire for epicene women, his yellow eyes,[10] and his satyr-like qualities. That Jones is a foundling anticipates Popeye and Joe Christmas, and perhaps harks back to such literary antecedents as Tom Jones and Oliver Twist, the former being as concupiscent as Januarius Jones and the latter resembling Faulkner's character in having received his surname in accordance with an alphabetical scheme.

Soldiers' Pay also bears an indirect relationship to *Ulysses* in that the framework of each employs the same classical model, the *Odyssey*. Although the parallels in *Soldiers' Pay* remain intermittent and suggestive rather than dominant, they appear to be quite deliberate and, once again, the differences between Joyce's methods and Faulkner's are as illuminating as the parallels. In a sense, Faulkner picks up where Joyce leaves off: for Joyce, the travels of Odysseus on the way to Ithaca comprise the major source of interest; Faulkner, on the other hand, makes short work of the journey home of his Odysseus-figure, Donald Mahon, and concentrates on the social repercussions which attend his arrival.

The *Odyssey* has become, of course, the literary paradigm of a soldier returning from the wars, and the correspondences with the *Odyssey* in *Soldiers' Pay* constitute one strand of a complex network of classical allusions which serve to counterpoint the contemporary setting of the novel. The brief dialogues between

'Achilles' and 'Mercury'—the one serving as a prologue to the novel proper and the other occurring at the beginning of the fifth chapter—imply a comparison between the golden age of Homer's noble Achaeans and the plight of the modern soldier. The debasement of the heroic martial tradition, and the concomitant inversion of traditional roles—perhaps hinted at in Jones's sarcastic reference to Donald as 'Mercury's brother' (135)—constitutes one of the primary features of the parallel drawn between Odysseus and Donald. Like Odysseus, Donald's single most distinctive feature is a scar: Odysseus receives his scar while on a successful boar hunt; Donald receives his in the course of an unprofitable mission during World War I. And whereas the sight of Odysseus's scar brings the joy of recognition to his father and Eurycleia, Donald's scar disfigures his face almost beyond recognition and sickens his father and friends.

Odysseus survives the Trojan War and the journey back to Ithaca relatively intact thanks largely to the benevolent intervention of Athene. Donald in *Soldiers' Pay* is a pitiful Odysseus, and his Athene, Margaret Powers, fails miserably in her task of seeing that the hero returns safely and drives out the usurpers who are taking advantage of the hospitality of his home. Athene, the Greek goddess of war, is referred to in the *Odyssey* as 'Hope of Soldiers'[11] and it accords with the ironic tone of the correspondences in *Soldiers' Pay* that the Athene-figure should have 'Powers' as a surname by marriage and that she should nonetheless be as much a victim as is Donald himself of a war over which she has had no control.

As with Odysseus, Donald's family and friends presume him to be dead, and his father, like Laertes in the *Odyssey*, has withdrawn from public life and devoted himself to his garden. Two characters, Cecily and Emmy, share the role of Donald's Penelope; Cecily, however, is neither faithful nor wise and at the very moment of Donald's return is embracing one of her many suitors, George Farr. Cecily's parallel with Penelope may be hinted at in the drugstore scene in Chapter 6, when she tells George, 'Oh, no. I can't come back this afternoon. I have some sewing to do' (216). Given Cecily's personality, this excuse seems rather implausible; nevertheless, it does recall the loom trick which Penelope uses to forestall the suitors in the *Odyssey*, as does the fact that Emmy, in one sense Donald's true Penelope, initially 'got a job sewing for a dressmaker' (128) after Donald's departure for the war. Donald's lacking the strength to hold either of these Penelope-figures indicates one of the essential ironies of his position as the Returned Hero: George Farr may be Donald's Antinous, but Donald—whose name means 'proud chief'—is utterly incapable of driving away either Farr himself or even that basest of suitors, Januarius Jones.

Once Donald returns, Emmy takes care of him, functioning in this respect in much the same manner as does Odysseus's faithful nurse, Eurycleia, and sharing the role with Mammy Cal'line. Despite their ministrations, however, Donald is doomed to die. The climax of the *Odyssey* occurs in Book XXIII when Odysseus and Penelope are reunited in bed. The inversion of this scenario in *Soldiers' Pay* becomes apparent when one of Donald's Penelope-figures is seduced by George Farr and the other by Jones, while Donald himself is committed to a marriage which for its brief duration must, of course, remain unconsummated. One of the more striking ironies in the *Odyssey* is that the very day on which the suitors plan to celebrate the marriage of one of their number to Penelope becomes instead the day of their deaths at the hands of Odysseus. Faulkner reverses this irony by having Donald, the Odysseus figure, buried shortly after his marriage.

A primary element in Odysseus's vanquishing of the suitors, and one of his dominant character traits throughout the *Odyssey*, is his ability to use language effectively, a talent which enables him to manipulate circumstances; Donald's almost total silence by comparison constitutes Faulkner's comment on an age which has lost its voice and consequently remains victimized by contingencies. Inherent in Odysseus's capacity for generating fictions concerning himself, however, is the danger that he may ultimately lose his identity entirely: just as Donald's lack of verbal dexterity prohibits him from identifying himself when he returns to Charlestown, so does Odysseus's protean facility in creating roles become a threat to his retention of a firm sense of self. Douglas Stewart has suggested that Odysseus's major problem upon his return to Ithaca involves the need to forsake his guise as Nobody and assert himself once again as Odysseus.[12] This seems, *mutatis mutandis*, the approximate position of Donald Mahon: his loss of identity is implicit in his lack of verbal response, in his failure to recognize figures from his past, and in the loss of all of his papers 'save only a certificate of discharge from a British hospital' (114). For both Odysseus and Donald, the use of language plays a significant part in the restoration of identity: the former declares his true name to the suitors, the latter re-establishes his relationship with his father by telling him 'That's how it happened' (294).

Given the inversions in the correspondences between Odysseus and Donald, it seems appropriate that while Odysseus's assertion of his identity enables him to rout the suitors and bring order back to Ithaca, the restoration of Donald's identity only allows him to die. As the specialist from Atlanta tells Margaret, Donald 'should have been dead these three months were it not for the fact that he seems to be waiting for something. . . . He remembers nothing of his life before he was injured' (154–155). Thus Donald's objective in life, to borrow the phrase of Addie Bundren's father, is 'to get ready to stay dead' and, as the specialist's diagnosis indicates, Donald will have to 'lie dying' until he regains his memory and thereby his identity.[13]

Because of his injury, Donald inhabits a world where time is non-existent, a nether sphere partaking fully neither of life nor of death. As Faulkner's short story 'All the Dead Pilots' demonstrates, Faulkner considered Donald's situation to typify that of the World War I aviators who in one sense survived, but in another, perhaps more important, respect all died on 11 November 1918. The returned veterans in *Soldiers' Pay* suffer from deracination and dislocation, and the experience of war has resulted in their being relegated to a spectral realm on the periphery of community life, moving like disembodied shades engaged in a futile attempt to re-establish some sense of personal identity.

Faulkner further intimates that the residents of Charlestown are themselves afflicted with a similar malaise. Although Charlestown appears on the surface to be placid, conventional, 'normal', in fact its surfaces are unstable, certainties are lost, personal identities are mutable or non-existent, the inner voices of the members of the community contradict their public statements, they exchange roles and become ghostly and phantasmagoric. Indeed, Charlestown comes to resemble Eliot's London in *The Waste Land*, an 'unreal city' in which the spiritually dead antic the motion of life while remaining unaware of their own moribundity. Hence, Donald's physical condition relates directly to the spiritual plight of the community, and Margaret's reference to the veterans at the dance as 'sitting there like lost souls waiting to get into hell' (196) applies equally to everyone else in Charlestown, including Margaret herself. Margaret, the Athene-figure who should ensure the restoration of vitality to a spiritually stagnant community, instead remains death-oriented throughout the novel, all of her actions being predicated upon a need to exorcise the spirit of her dead husband. In marrying Donald, she in a sense weds death and thereby ensures the repetition of that pattern established with her previous husband, Dick, of a hasty marriage followed shortly by the death of her spouse.

As her interior monologues suggest, Margaret fears sexuality and the commitment which responsible sexual activity entails, an attitude widely prevalent in Charlestown as a whole. The dance at Mrs Wardle's which Margaret describes as a 'hell' (196) assumes for the reader the nightmarish quality of a *danse macabre*, in part because the dancers simulate sexual response without hope of contact or fulfillment. In a manner suggestive of Jones's 'chaste Platonic nympholepsy' (225), those at the dance implicitly advocate desire without satisfaction, sexual attraction without carnal activity. Consequently, George Farr's exclusion from these phantasmic revels is appropriate: even though other aspects of his attitude invite condemnation, he at least exhibits a more vital sexual response than do most of his fellow townspeople.

George's fervor is not, however, shared by its recipient, Cecily Saunders. Much of the attention in the dance episode focuses on Cecily, the embodiment of the attenuated and jaded sexual attitudes of the community. Throughout *Soldiers' Pay*, the two salient aspects of Cecily's characterization are her sexual allure and her essential insubstantiality: so an unidentified girl at the dance tells her, 'See right through you. Stay out of the light' (205) and Gilligan twice makes similar comments (208, 211). The confluence of alluring and epicene elements in Cecily exerts a powerful influence upon all the males in the novel, including Januarius Jones. When Jones and Cecily are on the couch in the Saunders home, he mentally remarks upon her 'unseen face nimbused with light and her body, which was not body, crumpling a dress that had been dreamed', and then tells her, 'If I really held you close you'd pass right through me like a ghost, I am afraid' (224). Cecily's attraction thus corresponds to the community's sterile demand for an unattainable figure of desire and her habitual wearing of diaphanous clothing caters to this inherently life-denying impulse. That these clothes are usually white serves to associate her with the White Woman in Faulkner's early poem, 'Lilacs', who is apparently a figure of death. Like the mourning that Margaret wears, Cecily's attire signifies the close relation of sex and death in

Soldiers' Pay: they are not only 'the front and the back door' (295) of existence, but in the 'unreal city' of Charlestown they become virtually identical.

The curiously unlocalized presentation of Charlestown provides the setting with a universality signifying that the attitudes characteristic of this small Southern town persist in the post-war world in general. 'Charles' means 'man' and the similar plight of all the inhabitants of this microcosm suggests an all-pervasive malaise: almost every major character in the novel is described at some point as 'sick' or 'ill'. The fact that the doctors who examine Donald remain ineffectual in their attempts to cure him, or even to alleviate his pain, indicates the essential futility of the society's efforts to salve the wounds of war, and the Rector's remark that Donald would have made a marvelous surgeon (68) suggests the extent to which the war has precluded the possibility of youth's providing a regenerative cure for the ills of society.

Indeed, some aspects of Donald's infirm condition seem to be epidemic in Charlestown. For example, the profuse references to faulty vision which permeate *Soldiers' Pay* indicate that most of the characters in some sense share Donald's blindness, the implication, in part, being that these members of the community have shut their eyes to the grim effects of the war. The Rector's persistent delusion that his son will recover and his scar be removed epitomizes this tendency. The Rector's expressed desire to spend his retirement reading in the garden until overtaken by blindness associates his willed innocence with the physical blindness of his son and implies that his obdurate refusal to dispense with his illusion becomes as debilitating and restrictive as his son's near-comatose condition. Donald's brief recovery of sight, significantly enough, depends upon his remembering the manner in which his gruesome wound was inflicted.

The somewhat problematic first chapter of *Soldiers' Pay* indicates the extent of this impulse to evade the circumstances brought about by the war. Most of the passengers aboard the train either ignore or patronize the returning soldiers, thus anticipating the attitude adopted by those in Charlestown. The conversations of the soldiers themselves in the first chapter also reflect the universal spiritual attenuation resulting from the war: the banter between Gilligan and Lowe in which each refers to the other by a variety of military ranks which neither in fact possesses, Gilligan's references to the conductor as 'the admiral' and to the porter as

'George', 'Claude', and 'Othello', and Donald's parrot-like repetition of names, including his own—all register a general loss of the perception of individuation and serve to characterize a world in which sexual, personal, and social identities are blurred.

As the numerous incidents involving mistaken identity in *Soldiers' Pay* make clear, almost every character in the novel suffers from some form of identity confusion, and most adopt superficial but socially acceptable roles as a substitute for self-definition. Even Joe Gilligan, who in certain ways is the most stable character in this world of flux, initially assumes the persona of 'Yaphank' in order to play out the role of returned veteran. Faulkner apparently had Gilligan's role-playing in mind when he systematically deleted the references to 'Gilligan' in the first section of the first chapter in the Berg typescript for *Soldiers' Pay*, substituting either personal pronouns or the nickname 'Yaphank'.[14] That Gilligan's actions in the first section are inconsistent with his attitude throughout the remainder of the novel appears to be precisely the point which Faulkner wished to emphasise: aboard the train in the first section Gilligan adopts the persona of Yaphank and, in one sense, it is a measure of his essential integrity that he quickly drops the role and begins to act like Joe Gilligan, to be in every sense himself. In the second section of Chapter 1, Gilligan makes a point of impressing his name upon Lowe, even going to the extent of spelling it aloud for him. This assertion of personal, as opposed to military, identity demonstrates Gilligan's ability to confront the ramifications of the war and thereby dispense with them. This capacity for putting the war behind him—an ability which none of the other characters in *Soldiers' Pay* quite seems to possess—should be read favorably insofar as it represents an early instance of Faulkner's insistence on the necessity of living fully in the present.

Yet in many ways Gilligan seems more appealing in the opening chapter than in the remainder of the novel, and the dissipation of his vitality may be related to Faulkner's use of *Soldiers' Pay* as a vehicle for the investigation of his own role as artist. The highly allusive content of 'Yaphank's' remarks—he refers in passing, for example, to Coleridge's *The Rime of the Ancient Mariner* and Shakespeare's *Hamlet*—and the verbal play in which he engages suggest that Gilligan has some rudimentary potential as an artist of sorts, but precisely because he rejects this alternative persona his potential remains unrealized. Conversely, the fledgling poet Januarius

Jones is too facile in his capacity to shift roles and therefore also compromises his position as a potential artist.

As Millgate observes, Faulkner throughout his apprenticeship was experimenting with different fictional guises to try to determine his own direction as a writer.[15] The abundant references to the reading done by the various characters indicate that *Soldiers' Pay* concerns itself, in part, with an exploration of the process and objective of the literary endeavor. As in the other non-Yoknapatawpha novels, the quality of understanding which the characters in *Soldiers' Pay* bring to a given work, their integrity as readers, emerges as being far more important than the range of their reading and constitutes an index by which their worth may be measured. Jones and Gilligan can be seen, in these terms, as two muted artist-figures whose diametrically opposed approaches to reading signify two variant attitudes toward the nature and function of language itself.

Referring to another Faulkner artist-figure, Ernest V. Trueblood, Michael Grimwood has observed that Trueblood's 'convertibility' from the dilettantish prig of 'Afternoon of a Cow' into a 'dull Texas farmer, as in [the screenplay] "One Way to Catch a Horse", suggests that the rube and the fop are simply two opposite results of the same self-parodic urge, resulting from two opposite reactions—a "low" one and a "high" one—against the middling life of Oxford'.[16] This 'self-parodic urge' may be traced from Faulkner's earliest writings and certainly appears in his first novel, *Soldiers' Pay,* the characterization of Jones corresponding to what Grimwood terms Faulkner's 'high' reaction and that of Gilligan embodying his 'low' reaction.

Jones has a voracious appetite for reading, although his application of it is somewhat suspect. His use of literature as an aid to seduction recalls Faulkner's largely ironic account of his own discovery of poetry in the autobiographical essay 'Verse Old and Nascent: A Pilgrimage', which appeared in the New Orleans *Double Dealer* during the time when he was working on *Soldiers' Pay*:

> I was not interested in verse for verse's sake then. I read and employed verse, firstly, for the objective of furthering various philanderings in which I was engaged, secondly to complete a youthful gesture I was then making, of being 'different' in a small town.[17]

Not surprisingly, Faulkner notes that such an attitude impeded his perceiving the deeper meanings in poetry and that it was not until some time later—after his 'concupiscence' had waned, as he humorously put it—that he began to go beyond the 'bright and bitter sound' and grasp the truths conveyed by the verse itself. Jones, too, employs poetry both to further his 'philanderings' and to attempt to distinguish himself from the stagnant milieu of a small town. Yet he never progresses past this stage: as a reader, his development has been arrested by his subordination of meaning to motive. Nonetheless, Jones does try to bring his reading directly to bear on life, as seen in his use of literary citations when trying to explain to Cecily his concept of Platonic nympholepsy. Indeed, the rather feverish application of his reading for the objective of seduction provides one of the few sources of vitality in a generally moribund community.

Jones's nemesis, Joe Gilligan, would seem on the surface to be no match for Jones as a reader; yet the sincerity which the former brings to his reading aloud to Donald, his unselfish attempt to assuage the trauma of a virtual stranger's last days, contrasts markedly with the self-centered motives for Jones's reading. Unlike Silas Wegg in Dickens's *Our Mutual Friend,* Gilligan reads Gibbon aloud not for profit but out of compassion, as a form of therapy for the stricken veteran. His faltering attempts to extract meaning from the polysyllabic text highlight the sincerity of his effort both to comprehend the work itself and to palliate Donald's condition. The salutary effect of his ministrations is suggested by his being referred to as 'Doctor' Gilligan on two occasions (157, 285), which suggests a contrast between his successful efforts to provide comfort to Donald and the negligible effects of the medical doctors who examine the young serviceman. The references to 'Doctor' Gilligan also present a reversal of the way in which the references to the Rector by his title of 'Doctor' (115, 117) actually highlight his ineffectuality in caring for his son. Gilligan's unwittingly vanquishing Jones in repartee, leaving the latter feeling like 'a swordsman who has been disarmed by a peasant with a pitchfork' (289), testifies to the power of Gilligan's compassionate humanity and to the esteem accorded it by Faulkner himself.

While Gilligan's motives are pure, his timidity with language poses an obstacle both to his reading and to his attempts to define his position in Charlestown. The virtual disappearance of the allusive, comic, and creative characteristics of his discourse after the first section of *Soldiers' Pay* demonstrates that his adamant assertion of personal identity becomes so inflexible as to exclude much of his potential for adaptation and imaginative growth. While in New Orleans, Faulkner himself cultivated the dress and mannerisms of the returned veteran and created elaborate fictions to reinforce that image. That this disappearance of Gilligan's verbal vitality coincides with his disavowal of the role of Yaphank may signify Faulkner's recognition that an author must of necessity be a creator of roles, of characters, and that a rigid adherence to a single outlook results in the stultification and, in fact, the disintegration of the creative impulse.

Although Faulkner advocates a certain degree of flexibility in the author's response to his world, his presentation of Jones makes clear that the artist must not forsake personal integrity in order to accommodate the demands of his audience: he must remain adaptable without allowing his perspective to become diffuse. As in the implicit comparison between Donald Mahon and Odysseus, one might say that Gilligan's inarticulateness, his lack of experience with language and fictions, renders him incapable of authoring himself in relation to the world, while Jones's verbal facility, his Janus-like propensity for switching roles instantaneously, results not in a consolidation but in a fragmentation of the self-generated fiction of personal identity.

In an introduction which he wrote for *The Sound and the Fury* in the early thirties, Faulkner's analysis of his own approach to writing after he had completed *Soldiers' Pay* suggests a combination of the divergent attitudes towards language exhibited by Gilligan and Jones:

> I had learned a little about writing from Soldiers' Pay—how to approach language, words: not with seriousness so much, as an essayist does, but with a kind of alert respect, as you approach dynamite; even with joy, as you approach women: perhaps with the same secretly unscrupulous intentions.[18]

In the process of writing *Soldiers' Pay*, that is to say, Faulkner discovered that the positive aspects of the positions on language respectively embodied in Gilligan and Jones were equally requisite to his own literary creed: the author must approach words warily and humbly, always aware of their potency, yet at the same time he must not shrink from grappling with words, exploiting them, in order to convey meaning most effectively. In *Soldiers' Pay* Faulkner implies that the writer's first obligation resides in that writer's own ethical and artistic criteria; yet, if the fictions created are to have lasting value, they must at the same time transmit the truths of the human heart to the reader, to elicit if need be that grief which grieves on universal bones to which Faulkner was later to refer in the Nobel Prize Address.[19]

The tension and complexity resulting from the interplay of the author's own exacting standards and the realization of the crucial necessity and inevitable failure of language to express ideas fully, to recapture presence, is one of the most compelling features of Faulkner's work and constitutes a primary topic of discussion in *Mosquitoes,* the novel which immediately follows *Soldiers' Pay.* In *Soldiers' Pay,* as later in *Mosquitoes,* Faulkner implies rather than describes an authentic attitude for the artist and suggests approval of some aspects of a character's perspective while intimating that other features are flawed.

Perhaps the most severely qualified artist-figure in *Soldiers' Pay* is the Rector, who uses language to placate both his congregation and himself, to evade and mollify rather than to explore and express. The spiritual complacency of the sermon which the Rector prepares on the Biblical passage, 'The Lord is my shepherd: I shall not want' (152), consequently pales by comparison with the hymn sung by the blacks in their dilapidated church—'Feed Thy Sheep, O Jesus'—which signifies 'All the longing of mankind for a Oneness with Something, somewhere' (319). In the person of the Rector, Faulkner demonstrates the insufficiency of the writer's placidly accepting Candide's dictum and merely cultivating his own garden; rather, he must move out of himself, experience the world, and relate the complexities attendant upon that experience as faithfully as possible.

The Rector's primary work of art is his garden which, like all artifacts, serves as a substitute for presence; the Rector, however, uses his garden not to come to terms with the pain generated by Donald's absence, but to deny it. Whereas the responses of Jones and Gilligan to language and life are equally invalid because each in its polarity excludes the other, the Rector evades response entirely by retreating into a world of willed illusion. That the Rector's garden does not necessarily conform to his idealistic conception of it may be indicated by the fact that his library contains a copy of *Paradise Lost* which Jones peruses while awaiting the

Rector's arrival (136). Nevertheless, the Rector's garden literally becomes for him his wife and son, and the description of his face as looking like 'a murdered Caesar's' (294) when he is finally forced to confront the imminence of Donald's death derives much of its impact from the reader's sense that the Rector is his own assassin, that he has been self-betrayed by his inauthentic use of the creative imagination to withdraw from life rather than to face it. His capitulation to 'circumstance' in the final chapter reveals the fundamental flaws in the fictions he has created to insulate himself from the world, and emphasises the extent to which he constitutes not only a moral but an imaginative vacuum in *Soldiers' Pay*.

The aggregation of elements pertaining to the role of the artist in *Soldiers' Pay* suggests that Faulkner's own future course as a novelist was as yet undetermined. That no one of the characters in *Soldiers' Pay* exhibits a satisfactory approach to language reflects the young Faulkner's high standards and implies that he was himself searching, albeit through the use of negative examples, for some positive construction of his future role. This concern with the genesis and ramifications of literature, with the crucial importance of the artist's approach to his material and his craft, was to absorb Faulkner for the remainder of his career and represents one of the most prominent features of the non-Yoknapatawpha novels as a group. More immediately, the significance of art, for both artist and audience, was to be explicitly and exhaustively investigated in his next novel.

3

Mosquitoes

Although *Mosquitoes*, Faulkner's second novel, is often considered to be his least significant work, that is a judgment which will seem damning only to those who underestimate all the other works in the canon. Whatever its strengths and weaknesses may in fact be, the novel remains a fascinating document for an understanding of the ideas, assumptions and ambitions with which Faulkner started out in the twenties and of the stages by which he came so astonishingly into his own. *Mosquitoes* occupies a pivotal position in the canon, immediately preceding the beginning of Faulkner's exploration of his mythical county, Yoknapatawpha. Constituting an extensive exploration of art and the role of the artist, *Mosquitoes* thereby assumes particular importance as an expressive index of Faulkner's aesthetics at this critical point in his career.

Like his earlier novel *Soldiers' Pay*, which dealt with the popular twenties theme of post-war disillusionment, *Mosquitoes*, cast in the mold of the 'novel of ideas', involves a rather self-conscious attempt to follow the track of contemporary fiction. It is quite possible that Faulkner's dissatisfaction with the results of these experiments in literary contemporaneity provided part of the impetus for his delving into his own 'little postage stamp of native soil': in 1928, looking back from the vantage point of the fictional county which he came to call Yoknapatawpha, he could refer to *Soldiers' Pay* as 'youngly glamorous' and to *Mosquitoes* as 'trashily smart'.[1]

One of the central concerns of *Mosquitoes* is the extent to which language reflects, distorts, subsumes or creates life. Faulkner's concern with language in *Mosquitoes* has often been noted, most commentators assserting that he protests against the debasement of language resulting when words are divorced from action. A corollary of this position has, however, been largely ignored: in this novel Faulkner also suggests the awesome power of words, exploring the relationship between language and literature, and that between literature and life. That the word 'mosquitoes' itself is never mentioned in the text proper serves as an oblique indication of the innate potency of the Word—it becomes conspicuous by its very absence and thereby functions indirectly to reinforce this central theme.

The discussions aboard the *Nausikaa* relating to language and art have generally been dismissed as tedious and inconsequential, but such a view results primarily from a perception of Gordon as Faulkner's ideal artist and a consequent acceptance of his negative evaluation of the conversations. It seems unlikely, however, that Faulkner would have devoted such a large proportion of the novel to discussions about art if his intention were merely to dismiss them offhand. Rather the remarks on the process and objective of writing fiction reflect back upon preceding action and description, anticipate future developments, and offer above all an avenue through which *Mosquitoes* itself may be approached. No one of the various views on art presented by the characters within the novel, however, receives complete authorial sanction. Every character in *Mosquitoes* explicitly or implicitly evinces a different attitude towards language and each may be placed on a scale the opposite extremes of which are Talliaferro's belief that the word is all and Gordon's dismissal of language as irrelevant and insubstantial.

Gordon's contempt for discussion of any sort emerges as one of his most pronounced characteristics. He rarely speaks himself and his interior monologues indicate that he holds no brief for those who do: 'Talk, talk, talk: the utter and heartbreaking stupidity of words. It seemed endless, as though it might go on forever. Ideas, thoughts, became mere sounds to be bandied about until they were dead'.[2] Gordon's attitude, however, does not necessarily correspond to Faulkner's own. The former's occupation as a sculptor renders him capable to a certain extent of dispensing with language as a primary mode of expression; Faulkner himself, on the other hand, recognized as early as 1925 that words were his 'meat and bread and drink'.[3] Furthermore, the limitations to Gordon's capacity for perception are exposed in the Prologue: he ignores Talliaferro who, although something of a buffoon, is eventually shown to have some potential as a subject for artistic development; more explicitly, he disregards Mrs Maurier in favor of her self-centered niece, Patricia Robyn. The Prologue's hints of the suffering concealed behind Mrs Maurier's social mask tend to confirm the sense of Gordon's artistic myopia, and despite his later creation of the clay bust of Mrs Maurier—an artifact which in terms of sheer artistic accomplishment must be interpreted favorably—his actions throughout the novel as a whole serve to intensify the mixed feelings with which the reader regards his artistic approach. Gordon's aloof behavior results in his seeming 'haughty and inhuman almost' (152), his extreme arrogance is noted time and again, and his eyes are twice described as resembling those of a surgeon (24, 154). His 'bedside manner' when he finally examines Mrs Maurier's face appears to be not only tactless but brutal, indicating that when garnering materials for his art he can be as heedless of the feelings of others as is his secret-sharer, Josh Robyn.

While Gordon does not seem to be deliberately cruel, he does wilfully divorce himself from all forms of social interaction and revel in his arrogant loneliness. Once aboard the yacht, a setting in which social interchange is almost inevitable, he becomes more or less invisible both to the reader and to the other members of the yachting party, as is emphasised by the consternation and mystery surrounding his disappearance. That Gordon's absence remains unnoticed until quite some time after the fact suggests that he is not after all the focus of attention in the novel. One might say that while aboard the *Nausikaa* Gordon lacks articulation as a character because he lacks the inclination to articulate—that he refuses to define himself within the context of a novel in which characterization depends so heavily upon each character's verbalization. Hence, in *Mosquitoes* Faulkner hints at a correlation between language as self-expression and language as self-definition.

Gordon's failure, or refusal, to express himself in words negatively influences his relationship with Patricia: his inability to relate the fable of Halim and the king, for example, runs contrary to his purposes, assuming that he does in fact desire Patricia herself and not merely his idealized conception of her. His reticence seems even more damning in that the fable itself, reminiscent of the tales of the *Arabian Nights*, underscores the necessity for verbal communication by its indirect allusion to Shazarad, whose survival quite literally depends upon her ability to tell stories.

Gordon's detachment and arrogance are not only self-defeating in his personal relationships but also threaten the integrity of his art. Patricia's advice to him after his return to the *Nausikaa* serves as an accurate, if crude, assessment of his problem: 'You ought to get out of youself. You'll either bust all of a sudden some day, or just dry up. . . .' (270—Faulkner's ellipsis). Faulkner's play on the meanings of the word 'bust' in Patricia's statement anticipates Gordon's creation of the clay bust of Mrs Maurier and hints at the necessity of Gordon's finding some means of authentic artistic expression before his intensity and his talent do indeed 'dry up'.

Gordon's other work of art, the marble statue, embodies his refusal to sully himself with personal interaction, its purity depending upon its insularity from human experience, its armlessness and leglessness aptly representing the truncation of his artistic perspective. It is his 'feminine ideal: a virgin' (26), and given the detrimental effects of prolonged abstinence on Mrs Maurier and Talliaferro, it becomes evident that Gordon's ideal denies basic human compulsions. Even his immunity to the ravages of the mosquitoes—symbols, as Brooks notes, of the intrusion of reality upon illusion[4]—emphasises Gordon's isolation and impregnable idealism.

Gordon's unorthodox lifestyle reinforces his alienation. Although used by Faulkner to underline the triviality of the social concerns of Talliaferro and Mrs Maurier, Gordon's disdain for convention becomes suspect precisely because it is too stereotypically bohemian, fulfilling Mrs Maurier's—and, to a certain extent, even Hooper's—notion of the way in which an artist should live. Fairchild recognizes the danger of Gordon's isolation, and his comment upon it in the Prologue anticipates Patricia's later remark: 'He ought to get out of himself more. . . . You can't be an artist all the time. You'll go crazy' (51). Fairchild himself suffers from no such problem, and Julius notes the discrepancy between Fairchild's gregarious temperament and Gordon's proclivity for self-containment:

> 'outwardly you [Fairchild] might be anything. You are an artist only when you are telling about people, while Gordon is not an artist only when he is cutting at a piece of wood or stone. And it's very difficult for a man like that to establish workable relations with people.' (51)

In a sense, Julius is exactly right when he mentions to Fairchild: 'Gordon hasn't served his apprenticeship yet, you know. You've got through yours' (43). Gordon's haughtiness and reticence should be viewed as the hallmarks of an immature artist. Joyce W. Warren has noted affinities between Gordon in *Mosquitoes* and Stephen Dedalus in *A Portrait of the Artist as a Young Man,*[5] and these presumably deliberate parallels further suggest Gordon's inadequacies as an artist. Joyce once remarked to Frank Budgen that most commentators on *A Portrait* ignored the second part of the title, with its insistence that Stephen was a portrait of the artist as a *young* man.[6] The misreading of Stephen as Joyce's ideal artist resembles current misconceptions concerning Gordon in *Mosquitoes*. Both characters have much potential as artists, but the question as to whether this potential will ever be realized remains open: Stephen's grandiloquent diary entries just prior to his departure from Ireland project an ambiguity about his future much like that developed in *Mosquitoes* by Gordon's creation of the 'virgin torso' and by his later embracing the prostitute.

That the yacht in Faulkner's novel is named *Nausikaa* may suggest the influence of *Ulysses*, and one might even speculate that the characterization of Gordon and Fairchild approximates that of Stephen and Bloom: Gordon resembles Stephen in terms of talent, loneliness, and arrogance; Fairchild recalls Bloom in being kind, solicitous, a bit befuddled, and sincere—to borrow a distinction which Joyce made in regard to Bloom, not so much good as decent.[7] Sherwood Anderson served as a model for Fairchild, a character who, as Edwin Arnold has observed, deserves more sympathy than he is usually accorded.[8] For example, Fairchild not only distinguishes himself from the others on the yacht by his capacity for human concern, but he is also credited with the creation of the Jackson stories which, significantly enough, find their source in earlier 'texts' resulting from the collaboration of Faulkner himself and Anderson.[9] The varied reception of Fairchild's tall tales in *Mosquitoes* reflects more on their audience's capacity for perception than on the qualities of the yarns themselves. Fairchild also provides two other central tales, the one involving his rather pathetic college career and the other concerning the outhouse epiphany. In many respects, Fairchild embodies a more valid artistic approach than does Gordon, and it seems pertinent to the differences between the two that the 'little kind of black man' (144) named Faulkner whom Jenny encounters at Mandeville resembles Fairchild much more than he does Gordon. It is also notable that Fairchild instigates the greater part of the action on board the *Nausikaa* whereas Gordon remains a shadowy figure in the background.

Granted, much of this action seems purposeless. Somewhat like Vladimir and Estragon in Beckett's *Waiting for Godot*, the characters in *Mosquitoes* use various activities simply to pass the time: they drink, dance, swim, play bridge, coil ropes, and try to tug the yacht—all in a futile effort to evade the knowledge of their own vacuity. Nevertheless, the initiation of any form of physical movement in such a devitalized milieu deserves some measure of commendation. The activities which Fairchild orchestrates involve the entire community aboard the *Nausikaa*, are essentially harmless, and in many respects embody an extension of the central concerns of the discussions of art in the novel: Fairchild's investment of significance in actions meaningless in themselves parallels the essentially arbitrary assignation of value in the relationship between origin and word, a topic which Fairchild repeatedly explores in his conversation. His eventual acceptance of his own incredible 'tale of a tug' as authentic exemplifies the overwhelming power of language to transform the past and shape the present.

The ludicrous consequences of that acceptance as revealed in the attempt to dislodge the *Nausikaa* from the sandbar result from Fairchild's confusion over language as supplementation and language as presence. That is to say, he allows the distinction between fiction and reality—a distinction so evident, for instance, in the Jackson stories—to become obscured, so that his attempted formulaic transference of that fiction to life is, like the tall convict's analogous attempt in *The Wild Palms*, doomed to failure. This same confusion, with potentially graver consequences, informs Patricia's escapade with David: while trying to apply her verbal construction of Edenic bliss to actuality, to make reality conform to her idealized conception of it, she embroils herself and David in a desperate situation. The absymal failure of Talliaferro's magic 'Word' in his efforts at seduction also betrays the folly of imposing half-baked fictions on actual circumstances. The essential problem with the attitudes of Patricia, Fairchild, and especially Talliaferro is not that they divorce words from action, as so many commentators on the novel maintain; quite to the contrary, in fact, they wed the two, deny the essential difference between fiction and reality, and in so doing futilely attempt to span the unbridgeable gap between re-presentation and presence. Gordon makes the opposite mistake in assuming that because the values conferred upon language signs remain arbitrary, words are utterly devoid of significance. That Gordon's position is misguided may be suggested by the mutual attraction of—and the similarities between—Patricia and Gordon. The two are very much alike in their idealism and lack of consideration for others, they follow much the same route in their respective journeys through the swampland, and both are returned to the *Nausikaa* by the same foul-mouthed swamper.

The contrast between Gordon's haughty reserve and Fairchild's gregariousness demonstrates Faulkner's contention in *Mosquitoes* that an immersion in life is requisite to achieving integrity and vitality in art. As Fairchild puts it in the Epilogue:

> '[Art is] getting into life, getting into it and wrapping it around you, becoming a part of it. Women can do it without art—old biology takes care of that. . . . A woman conceives . . . . And bears . . . . But in art, a man can create without any assistance at all: what he does is his. A perversion, I grant you, but a perversion that builds Chartres and invents Lear is a pretty good thing.' (320)

The theory of art as an intensification of life in this passage relates to Fairchild's 'listening to the dark and measured beating of the heart of things' (339), and to his subsequent definition of genius as the 'Passion Week of the heart' (339), implying that this theory at least in part has Faulkner's tacit approval. Fairchild's association of parturition and artistic creation consolidates the affinities between life and art implied earlier in *Mosquitoes* and resembles Stephen's theory of 'postcreation' in *Ulysses*. Finally, Fairchild's reference to art as a kind of felicitous perversion reflects back upon a number of the discussions in the novel, most notably that which concerns Eva Wiseman's book of poetry, *Satyricon in Starlight*.

In that discussion, significantly enough, Fairchild defends Eva's work and modern poetry in general; and although Julius in his role of devil's advocate disparages the poetry in his sister's book, the others—even Mark Frost and Major Ayers—appreciate its merits. The poems attributed to Eva are the products of Faulkner's own apprenticeship period and the inclusion of them in *Mosquitoes*, somewhat like Joyce's assigning the villanelle in *A Portrait* to Stephen, seems to be both a testament to his confidence in their worth and a form of autocriticism in which his prose characters discuss his own talents as a poet. Fairchild's explanation in this episode of the circumstances necessitating his shift from poetry to prose fiction relates to the decision Faulkner himself had already made, and in the context of *Mosquitoes* Fairchild's account can be read as a reflection on Faulkner's own past as a poet and on his projected future as a novelist. Of course, it would be just as much of a mistake to assume that Fairchild is Faulkner's spokesman as to accept Gordon as his ideal artist. Rather, what *Mosquitoes* offers is a variety of competing perspectives on language and art, an exploration mirroring Faulkner's own lack of certainty about his future as a writer of prose fiction, a laying out of options and possible positions rather than a choice of any one of them.

The exploratory nature of *Mosquitoes* inheres in its characterization, style, and structure: none of the characters remains completely consistent, the style is self-consciously experimental, and the structure is much more fluid than it might initially appear to be. The inconsistency of the characters' attitudes emerges from the various discussions, and they are inconsistent in action as well, at least insofar as none of them except Gordon fits the stereotype assigned by the other characters. Eva, for example, wears the wrong type of garters (95), Dorothy listens to Chopin rather than to Grieg (182), and Fairchild, as Julius never tires of observing, acts like anything but the stereotypical artist.

One of the principal discussions in *Mosquitoes* centers on a dissatisfaction with rigidly consistent fictional characterization:

> 'In life, anything might happen; in actual life people will do anything. It's only in books that people must function according to arbitrary rules of conduct and probability; it's only in books that events must never flout credulity.' (181)

By having the characters in *Mosquitoes* denigrate consistency and by demonstrating how each is dissociated from conventional stereotypes, Faulkner creates a metafiction in which his characters indirectly comment on their own traits as fictional personages. The implicit endorsement of realism in characterization and the ramifications of that endorsement for Faulkner's future work become readily apparent if one contrasts, for example, the overtly symbolic presentation of Donald Mahon in *Soldiers' Pay* with the more naturalistic characterization of another war-damaged Faulknerian aviator, Bayard Sartoris, in *Flags in the Dust*, the next novel after *Mosquitoes*.

While the style in certain passages of *Mosquitoes* may seem gratuitously experimental, it does relate to the symbiotic relationship between the discussions aboard the yacht and the way in which they, and *Mosquitoes* as a whole, are conveyed to the reader: the search for a valid artistic approach in the discussions is reflected in the author's own attempts to devise the appropriate style which will contribute most tellingly to the contextual significance of those discussions. The dramatic format of the 'At Breakfast' episode in which the coterie aboard the *Nausikaa* discuss Gordon's mysterious disappearance provides an example of Faulkner's fusion of style and content: the lack of narrative transition heightens the tension of this scene, captures the confusion felt by the characters regarding the circumstances and time of Gordon's going overboard, demonstrates Gordon's ingrained tendency towards self-dramatization, and emphasises the 'staginess' of Josh and Patricia's apparently callow attitude towards death. Similarly, the potpourri of stylistic devices so prominent in the ninth section of the Epilogue—parenthetical narration, interior monologue, dialogue without inverted commas, and so on—evinces Faulkner's experimental eclecticism and portrays the intoxication of Gordon, Fairchild and Julius, while the italicized portions of the episode recall Gordon's fable of Halim and serve to imbue the drunken spree with a mythic, fabular significance.

The less immediately apparent fluidity of the structure accords with the more obvious variability of the style in *Mosquitoes*. The juxtaposition of the relatively mundane life on the yacht and the dire situation in which Patricia and David find themselves in the 'Third Day' section provides one indication of the flexibility of what might appear in the abstract as a fairly rigid structural scheme progressing relentlessly from the Prologue, through the hours of each of the four days, to the Epilogue.

Faulkner subtly relates the swampland adventure to the conversations concerning literature on the yacht by structuring the description of Patricia and David's trek in terms of literary allusion and archetypal imagery. One possible source for the description is Aldous Huxley's *Those Barren Leaves,* which Faulkner had read prior to beginning work on *Mosquitoes*.[10] In Huxley's novel, Cardan leaves the sanctuary of Mrs Aldwinkle's palace in search of a statue, becomes lost in the mosquito-infested lowlands, and encounters Elver who is trying to murder his idiot sister by exposing her to what he hopes are malaria-carrying mosquitoes. Sinclair Lewis's 1914 novel *Our Mr. Wrenn* may also have contributed to the episode in *Mosquitoes*. Having left a party at which artistic types had congregated, the timid, self-deprecating Wrenn and his adventurous female companion Istra decide, at Istra's instigation, to take a train out of London and then hike to Aengusmere. Their preparations for the outing are as haphazard as those of Patricia and David, and although Wrenn (like David, doglike in his devotion) attempts to make the hike as agreeable as possible—for example, by cooking breakfast for Istra just as David does for Patricia in Faulkner's novel—the length of the hike, the persistent rain, and Istra's progressively worsening temper make it a failure. They eventually take the train into Aengusmere where they are confronted by the very people whom they had hoped to escape by leaving London, so that their journey, like that of the young couple in *Mosquitoes*, is essentially circular.

Patricia resembles Istra both in her prompting of the attempted escape and in her hopelessly idealistic attitude towards it. Her swimming naked on the morning of their departure adds to the Edenic aura of the early hours of the day but, once ashore, harsh reality soon dispels her illusions. Shortly after she teases the snake, she is bitten by a mosquito and remarks: 'Gee, I'd forgotten about them' (172). The archetypal implications of this passage are clear: the initial description of the swampland as a primordial paradise reflects Patricia's naive idealism, but her encounter with the snake, which ignores her 'with a sort of tired unillusion' (171), and with the mosquitoes serves as a reminder that Patricia and David inhabit a fallen world and therefore remain subject to those irritating—and potentially devastating—aspects of postlapsarian existence which Patricia has conveniently 'forgotten'.[11]

It is at this point in the episode that Faulkner begins to juxtapose the increasingly serious predicament of Patricia and David to the activities of those aboard the yacht. Dividing his material into specific units of time, he devotes alternate sections to the young couple and to the artists, and then achieves an even more striking effect by assigning alternate passages within each section first to one group, then to the other.[12] On one level, this juxtaposition contrasts the minor annoyances of those aboard the *Nausikaa* with the desperate straits of the two runaways. On another level, however, the life and death circumstances confronted by Patricia and David both highlight the insularity of the artists' milieu and stress the intrinsic importance of the topics which they bandy about so frivolously.

One of the central topics of these exchanges relates to the apparently opposed concepts of universality and regionalism in art—an ostensible dichotomy which Faulkner himself ultimately resolved in and through the creation of Yoknapatawpha: his Yoknapatawpha fiction succeeds in being regional without becoming provincial and treats universal concerns while nevertheless remaining anchored in a specific locale. To some extent, Faulkner's solution synthesizes the antithetical positions adopted in *Mosquitoes* by Eva Wiseman and Dawson Fairchild, characters whose surnames signify their opposing perspectives. Eva holds that there are only two subjects worth writing about, love and death, but while this may be acceptable as a general theory it lacks specificity. Conversely, Fairchild's literary prescriptions remain too restrictive to be universally applicable. His feelings about his lack of a college degree and his heavy reliance on oft-told tales manifest his intellectual and artistic insecurity: as Julius observes, Fairchild needs 'a standard of literature that is international. No, not a standard, exactly: a belief, a conviction that his talent need not be restricted to delineating things which his conscious mind assures him are American reactions' (242–3).

These and other comments on Fairchild's tendencies as a writer suggest that his self-imposed limitations result in his writing being provincial rather than regional—an important distinction, especially since Faulkner himself was at this time leaning towards a regionalist aesthetic. The analyses of Fairchild's provincialism indicate Faulkner's awareness of the possible pitfalls of an overly self-conscious reliance for material on any particular milieu. His implicit endorsement in *Mosquitoes* of a middle ground between the two extremes embodied by Eva and Fairchild was later to influence the shape of the canon as a whole: in his subsequent works, the Yoknapatawpha novels demonstrate the efficacy of treating universals within a specifically defined social context, while the non-Yoknapatawpha novels serve to emphasise that the writer need not confine himself to such a well-defined region in order to deal effectively and honestly with the human condition.

Another fundamental question considered in the discussions in *Mosquitoes*, that of the binary properties of language, does not so readily yield a solution and, indeed, may be irresolvable: words signify everything and nothing. That Julius and Fairchild, in particular, oscillate from one pole of this dichotomy of language values to the other indicates both the centrality of the question and the impossibility of arriving at any facile resolution. Julius's exploration of the nature of the dilemma is much the more eloquent, but Fairchild, despite his fumbling manner of expression, seems to have a fuller understanding of its vital importance:

> 'Well, it is a kind of sterility—Words,' Fairchild admitted. 'You begin to substitute words for things and deeds . . . and pretty soon the thing or the deed becomes just a kind of shadow of a certain sound you make by shaping your mouth a certain way. But you have a confusion, too. I don't claim that words have life in themselves. But words brought into a happy conjunction produce something that lives, just as soil and climate and an acorn in proper conjunction will produce a tree.' (210)

While Fairchild recognizes the partial validity of viewing words as intrinsically meaningless—as Addie Bundren puts it in *As I Lay Dying*, as 'just the gaps in people's lacks'[13]—at the same time his reference to 'words brought into a happy conjunction' anticipates his later definition of that 'Passion Week of the heart' in which 'the hackneyed accidents which make up this world . . . brought together by chance in perfect proportions, take on a kind of splendid and timeless beauty' (339). Significantly enough, he offers to prove his contention that words have substance by reading from Eva's poetry.

Fairchild's career as a novelist has evidently provided him with much insight into the dilemma of the relative and arbitrary values of words, and of course the young Faulkner himself had a vested interest in the matter and in its implications for his future career. In *Mosquitoes* Faulkner also exhibits his awareness of the irony inherent in the very necessity of using words to investigate language; the absence of a metalanguage accounts for much of the 'confusion' to which Fairchild refers, as well as for many of the circumlocutions, repetitions, strained metaphors, and inconsistencies present in the discussions themselves. Ultimately, one supposes, Faulkner the budding novelist would have accepted some theory akin to Fairchild's 'childlike faith in the efficacy of words' (249) to resolve the ingrained paradox of language values and thereby avoid literary neurasthenia.

A related predicament appears in the discussions of art in general, art being variously viewed as a whimsical way of occupying time, as a perversion, as an esoteric enterprise of value only to those initiated into its sacred mysteries, as an endeavor which bears at best a merely tangential relation to life, as a means of seduction or revenge, and as the apex of human activity. As an artist, Faulkner may perhaps be assumed to have favored that last interpretation, but it is consistent with his later attitudes that he does not restrict art solely to conventional definitions of that term. Fairchild at one point defines art as anything that is done well (183), and his description of the 'Passion Week of the heart' embraces a wide range of reference—genius, that is to say, is capable of many manifestations. Julius likewise suggests that all people compose poetry in their youth, and some even write it down (249).

Faulkner's suggestion of the ubiquity of the artistic impulse—an ingredient, too, in his satire of the New Orleans coterie—appears in the projection as potential artist-figures of at least two characters, Major Ayers and Ernest Talliaferro, who lay no claim to such a status and are not taken seriously even as human beings by those who do. Although Ayers seems far removed from the world of art presented in *Mosquitoes*, his presumably spontaneous tall-tale of the absence of apple-tarts in Britain does constitute a worthy counterpart to Fairchild's relation of his first Jackson story, which it immediately follows. Hence, Julius's comment that Ayers embodies artistic potential may be less ironic than he realizes. Of course, the Major is a severely qualified artist-figure. His only direct comments on *Satyricon in Starlight* consist of a reference to it as 'that tweaky little book . . . . The syphilis book' (220), and his assertion that he appreciates the way modern publishers 'get their books up. Jolly, with colors, y' know' (208). His plan to market 'salts' to the American public equals in absurdity Gumbril's similar plan to mass-produce his inflatable 'patent small clothes' in Huxley's *Antic Hay*. Nevertheless, Ayers's sheer determination is a quality decidedly lacking in most of the more obvious artist-figures in Faulkner's novel. The only member of the group to do any private reading during the outing, his unsophisticated attempt to come to terms with *Satyricon in Starlight* is in some ways preferable to the vague generalizations on modern poetry offered by Fairchild and Julius.

Ayers also attempts to secure a sexual assignation with Jenny, an effort akin to Talliaferro's creeping up on her while she is asleep and trying to seduce her as she awakens. The others scoff at Talliaferro for trying to inveigle women with words, but their observations concerning the use of the written word to impress women indicate that they do much the same thing themselves. Fairchild disparagingly refers to Talliaferro's belief in using language for the purpose of seduction as 'the Great Illusion' (130), but Julius reminds him that he too—and everyone for that matter—indulges in one illusion or another:

> 'So don't you go around feeling superior to Talliaferro. I think his present illusion and its object [Jenny] are rather charming, almost as charming as the consummation of it would be—which is more than you can say for yours. . . . And so do you . . . so do you remember with regret kissing in the dark and all the tender and sweet stupidity of young flesh.' (131)

In spite of this perception, however, Talliaferro is largely ignored by the artists, including Gordon—with whom he is closely aligned in one way or another from the opening pages of the novel—and the author-typist in the last section of the Epilogue. Gordon has received much critical acclaim for his penetration to the sorrow lying beneath Mrs Maurier's mask of brittle volubility, but his failure to register a like potential in Talliaferro bears equal importance.

This neglect constitutes a particularly serious indictment because certain aspects of the presentation of Talliaferro imply that he is an informal member of the artists' guild. Early in the Prologue, Mrs Maurier asks Talliaferro if he too has become an artist, and although he replies that he contents himself with being merely a 'Maecenas' (18) the reader becomes aware by the conclusion of the novel that Talliaferro is himself an artist-figure.

Fairchild's definition of art as 'anything consciously done well . . . . Living, or building a good lawn mower, or playing poker' (183) relates to Faulkner's own association of the artist and the carpenter in later interviews as well as to his preference for playing the role of the backwoods farmer rather than that of the cosmopolitan literary lion. More directly, in the New Orleans sketch 'The Kid Learns' the narrator asserts: 'But more than this is being good in your own line, whether it is selling aluminum or ladies' underwear or running whiskey, or what. Be good, or die'.[14] Talliaferro in fact achieves a modest eminence in one of these lines of work: the reader discovers in the Prologue that, once having entered the women's clothing field, Talliaferro rose 'with comfortable ease to the position of wholesale buyer' (32).

Talliaferro is also the novel's most persistent creator of fictions.[15] These are generally rather self-aggrandizing scenarios in which he lives up to the appellation 'Don Juan' which Mrs Maurier gushingly bestows upon him in the Prologue; even so, the moment of inspiration for the most ambitious of these fictions is related in terms appropriate to artistic conception:

> He stopped utterly still in the flash of his inspiration. At last he had it, had the trick, the magic Word. It was so simple that he stood in amaze at the fact that it had not occurred to him before. . . . now that he had the key, now that he had found the Word, he dared admit to himself that he had suffered. (305–6)

Talliaferro's belief in the 'magic of words' constitutes in practical terms one of his primary flaws; it results, for example, in a predictable lack of success in his attempts at seduction. It is, however, an infatuation that would be appropriate to a writer, as is perhaps suggested by the fact that Fairchild's remarks on Talliaferro's employing language for the purpose of seduction echo a comment which Faulkner himself, prior to writing *Mosquitoes*, had made with reference to Keats: 'Keats trying to seduce Fanny Brawne with words' became a poet 'by accident'.[16] Talliaferro certainly fulfils, if only on a comic, reductive level, one of the standard Faulknerian requirements for the artist in that he is not destroyed by his grief but instead uses it to move out of himself and into the world, as Faulkner himself was perhaps trying to do in *Mosquitoes* with regard to his relationship with Helen Baird.[17]

Certain aspects of Talliaferro's personal history, in particular his fidelity to his invalid wife until her death, ought to induce sympathy and alert the reader to the possibility that there may be more to Talliaferro than his Prufrockian exterior would suggest. In the Epilogue, Fairchild briefly glimpses, but as quickly loses sight of, the 'hidden dark thing' (309) which lurks beneath Talliaferro's apparent superficiality. The reader should not, however, lightly pass over this revelation: the cumulative effect of the insights into Talliaferro's upbringing and outlook imply that his stilted attempts at communication and his inept striving for sexual fulfillment are in effect last-ditch efforts to establish contact with a world of experience denied to him through accidents of temperament, environment and, indeed, physical appearance.

The failure of the artists in *Mosquitoes* to understand, or even fully to recognize, Talliaferro's 'polite and hopeless despair' (309)—together with the implicit consequences of that failure—may be suggested by the italicized portions of section nine of the Epilogue. The beggar lying with the crust of bread in his hand is perhaps a Talliaferro-figure clutching his meager talent and desperate need in a world which ignores the existence of both. From this perspective, Talliaferro's reference to himself as a modern Maecenas can be read as an oblique intimation of his ability to 'support' the artists through his inherent potential as the basis for a fictional character—a potential which remains unrealized by the artists *in* the novel but not by the artist *of* the novel, Faulkner himself. Certainly the *'thin celibate despair'* (335) so often invoked in this section both provides an echo of the 'polite and hopeless despair' (309) earlier associated directly with Talliaferro and appropriately describes his general condition throughout *Mosquitoes*. The three gray, softfooted priests who pass by unheeding while the beggar dies in the street may well correspond to Gordon, Fairchild, and Julius, the three 'ministers' of art, as they stroll the by-ways of the Vieux Carré.

A variety of verbal echoes and shared images link this section of *Mosquitoes* with the roughly contemporary short story 'Carcassonne', which embodies in prose-poetic fashion one of Faulkner's seminal statements on the function of literature and the complexities of the artistic impulse.[18] In a typescript version of 'Carcassonne' Mrs Widdrington, the patron of the would-be poet in the garret, is named 'Mrs. Maurier',[19] and one can even imagine the poet lying under the tar-paper in the attic as Talliaferro himself, earnestly desiring *'to perform something bold and tragical and austere'*[20] but remaining incapable of doing so and dependent on his patron (or his future wife, Mrs Maurier) for even the most basic necessities. The rats stealing over the would-be poet's body in 'Carcassonne' correspond to those which scamper over the beggar in the *Walpurgisnacht* episode in *Mosquitoes;* and the reading of this beggar as a Talliaferro-figure could account for the similar correspondence between the poet's dialogue with his skeleton in the short story and the narrative description of Talliaferro in the Epilogue of the novel: 'he walked dark streets . . . feeling empty and a little tired and hearing his grumbling skeleton—that smug and dour and unshakable comrade who loves so well to say I told you so' (346).

Talliaferro's Prufrockian preoccupation with his age relates to the barrier between the young and their elders which figures prominently in *Mosquitoes* as a whole. Much has been made of the 'vitality' of youth in the novel, but a more pronounced characteristic common to the young people is an utter disregard for the feelings and property of others. For example, Josh makes no apology for—indeed, never even admits to—having dismantled the ship's steering mechanism; before replacing the pin in the mechanism, he cleans it with Talliaferro's toothbrush; his digging through Talliaferro's luggage looking for a rod resembles his twin sister's rifling the effects of the other women in search of money; and his sole reaction to Fairchild's moving and pathetic story of the fraternity debacle is 'You poor goof' (120). The vaunted vitality of the young people often leads to problematic consequences, in fact, and while Faulkner indicates that the young are no worse than their elders, he amply demonstrates that they are no better either. This disavowal of the cult of youthful innocence becomes even more apparent in *Flags in the Dust*, in which Virgil Beard, the young extortion-artist, blackmails Byron Snopes.

The single exception to the general lack of consideration among the young is David, the steward, and the contrast between him and Josh receives emphasis from the fact that the first words he speaks in the novel follow shortly after Josh's appraisal of Fairchild as a 'poor goof'. In many respects David seems superior to the older people on the yacht as well as to the younger set. He risks his life to save Major Ayers; he diligently attends to his duties; and, in contrast to the artists who take crude advantage of Mrs Maurier's hospitality, he does not even claim the wages she owes him before he leaves. Indeed, he displays some consideration for Mrs Maurier's feelings: in his note to Fairchild he asks him to give her the unintentionally transparent excuse that he is leaving the *Nausikaa* because he 'got a better job' (236). He also makes arrangements for the repayment of the five dollars which Fairchild had previously loaned to him.

Faulkner's attribution to David of some of his own recent experiences of European travel helps to consolidate the sense of qualified esteem for the character. Although it would be excessive to think of Faulkner as having identified with David, it does seem pertinent that the latter ultimately abandons his ideal woman, Patricia Robyn, the Helen Baird figure in the novel. Perhaps not coincidentally, in Anderson's 1925 short story 'A Meeting South' the character based on Faulkner is named David, and Faulkner himself used the name for a homespun artist-figure in the 'Out of Nazareth' sketch, also published in 1925. While the David of *Mosquitoes* is not one of the novel's self-proclaimed artists, he is one of the few characters to do any actual writing during the excursion, and his note to Fairchild exhibits a directness and simplicity, if not an orthography, which Fairchild and the others might do well to emulate. His escape from the stultifying group aboard the yacht approximates to Faulkner's own rejection of the New Orleans literary environment, and one can even read David's note to Fairchild as Faulkner's parodic farewell to Anderson:

> Dear Mr. Fairchild: I am leaveing the boat to day . . . tell Mrs. More I have got a better job ask her she will pay you [the] $5 dollars . . . you loned me. (236)

The promise of repayment was to be fulfilled in Faulkner's dedication to *Sartoris* and, much later, in his published memories of Anderson, while the 'better job' was to occupy him for the remainder of his career as a writer.

David seems the prime example of the single advantage youth has over age in *Mosquitoes*—the potential for development. Instead of adopting a simplistic dichotomy based on the relative ages of the characters in the novel, however, Faulkner uses youth and age as emblems of artistic perspective: in this sense, youth is the time of metaphor and acceptance, maturity that of simile and exclusion. According to Fairchild, one of the primary virtues of art lies in its capacity to remind us 'of our youth, of that age when life don't need to have her face lifted every so often for you to consider her beautiful. . . . And when it reminds us of youth, we remember grief and forget time. That's something' (319). While this statement in part results from Fairchild's mistaken exaltation of youth, it also aptly expresses the intensity of feeling necessary to, and generated by, a consummate work of art.

The celebration of grief as an affirmation of life is quintessentially Faulknerian, and Fairchild's statement anticipates Harry Wilbourne's declaration in *The Wild Palms*: '*Yes . . . between grief and nothing I will take grief.*'[21] Of crucial importance in Fairchild's assertion, given the corrosive properties of time, is the implicit function of memory as a tool in spanning the gap between experience and reflection, and between present and past. In *The Wild Palms,* Harry's memories of his and Charlotte's life together will affirm the principle of the value of experience through the very pain that they evoke; a like equation of the memory of grief and a full awareness of life is made explicit by Gordon in *Mosquitoes*: 'Only an idiot has no grief; only a fool would forget it. What else is there in this world sharp enough to stick to your guts?' (329). Although Gordon's personal dedication to this creed appears to be called into question by his heavy drinking and visit to the prostitute in section nine of the Epilogue—both presumably attempts to forget Patricia—the remark itself seems to carry authorial approval. Faulkner's concern with memory as integral to life coincides with his opinion that man must live in the present rather than be haunted by ghosts from the past, as his presentation of Quentin Compson in *The Sound and the Fury* and *Absalom, Absalom!* makes so abundantly clear. In all his treatments of this theme, he emphasises the importance not so much of the past itself but of the way in which the memory of that past is interpreted or expressed, thereby affecting one's present course of action. Life, for Faulkner, is motion, and the memory of grief provides a catalyst for that motion which is captured in—which is—art.

Faulkner's own memory of grief occasioned by the end of his relationship with Helen Baird apparently served as one motivation for the writing of *Mosquitoes*. The heavily autobiographical material in the novel, the ceaseless structural and stylistic experimentation, the discussions of the positive and negative aspects of various approaches open to the artist—these, taken together, mean that *Mosquitoes* embodies for the reader familiar with the subsequent canon neither a series of resolutions which the young Faulkner had formulated prior to the writing of the novel nor a demonstration of a firmly established artistic creed. Rather, as he was later to do in the three succeeding non-Yoknapatawpha novels, Faulkner in *Mosquitoes* examines various artistic positions, evaluating them in terms of possibility, integrity, and authenticity. At the same time, his inclination to incorporate aspects of himself into the presentation of such diverse figures as Talliaferro, David, and indeed the character named Faulkner indicates the intrinsic importance which the concerns dealt with in this work had for his own career as a novelist. Like the other non-Yoknapatawpha novels, *Mosquitoes* constitutes not a conclusion but an exploration whose results were to influence all of Faulkner's subsequent fiction. A line from Dylan Thomas's 'To-day, This Insect' may thus serve to characterize the crucial position of *Mosquitoes* within the Faulkner canon as a whole: 'The insect fable is the certain promise.'[22]

4
Pylon

By comparison with the amount of attention devoted to Faulkner's other works of the early thirties, *Pylon* has been largely neglected, and indeed the novel does seem to be an anomaly when considered within the context of the entire canon. Yet at the time that he was working on *Pylon*, Faulkner was producing some of his most significant works: *Light in August*, one of his finest novels, precedes *Pylon*, and *Absalom, Absalom!*, arguably his masterpiece, is *Pylon*'s immediate successor. Moreover, a number of Faulkner's fellow-writers held the book in high esteem when it was first published, and retained a favorable impression of it into their later years. In an early review in *Esquire*, for example, Ernest Hemingway stated that he had been 'reading and admiring *Pylon* by Mr. William Faulkner'[1] and in 1956 he wrote to a correspondent that *Pylon* and *Sanctuary* were Faulkner's 'most readable' works.[2] John Dos Passos, too, said in 1969 that he had 'read *Pylon* with great pleasure about the time it came out'.[3]

It seems appropriate that authors productive in the twenties and thirties should have appreciated the novel, for *Pylon*, like *Soldiers' Pay* and *Mosquitoes*, constitutes in many respects an exercise in literary contemporaneity, particularly in its resemblance to the 'social protest' novels which were being produced at the time by writers such as Dos Passos and Steinbeck. Economic differentiations and financial transactions emerge as primary motifs in *Pylon*, and the pointed distinction between the fliers' attitude towards money and that of, for instance, Feinman reveals a crucial aspect of the way in which they are distinguished from the society as a whole: the fliers' financial involvements tend to emphasise their fundamental humanity and sense of responsibility, while Feinman's underscore his greed and penchant for self-aggrandizement. Jiggs's use of Jack's winnings to buy a pair of boots for himself provides one example of the fliers' conscientiousness in monetary transactions: although the purchase itself seems an act of dubious propriety, Jiggs, having worn the boots once, refuses to wear them again until he has paid back the money—money which the troupe had apparently owed to him in the first place. The fliers as a group take money from the reporter's pocket as he lies inert on the doorstep, but they take only as much as they need and are scrupulous not only about informing him of the amount taken but also in keeping a running tab on the cash he gives them so that they can eventually repay the entire sum. Holmes's giving the reporter the money to ship Shumann's body home so that it will not be sent 'collect' further indicates their sensitivity.

The fliers' honorable conduct in financial matters conforms to the basic tenets of the social protest novel insofar as their lack of money causes them to recognize its worth in human terms. Their impoverishment, however, is not necessarily a virtue in itself, and it certainly makes them vulnerable to those who wield power in New Valois: they are utterly impotent when confronted with Feinman's unilateral decision to cut two and one-half percent out of each winner's fee. Jiggs's mistaken belief that the fliers intend to strike and the narrative description of their meeting with Feinman's representatives—'exactly that of the conventional conference between the millowners and the delegation from the shops'[4]—when combined with their absolute lack of power as a labor coalition illustrates their socio-economic enervation. The 'incorrigible insolvency' (9) of the fliers, combined with their 'irrevocable homelessness' (79), makes them completely dependent on each day's earnings for each night's lodging and precludes any possibility of their forming a union or even of organizing a 'wildcat' strike. The transiency and insolvency of the fliers are ironically implied by the very names of the two characters most responsible for providing the troupe with necessities: the homophonic pun on Jack's surname, 'Holmes', suggests one of the 'luxuries' which the fliers literally cannot afford, just as his first name is used elsewhere in *Pylon* as the slang equivalent for the money which the fliers so desperately lack; Shumann's first name, 'Roger', carries the irony of being a pilot's term for 'all right' or 'message received', while his surname seems equally telling in that the footwear of both Laverne and Jiggs leaves much to be desired.

Faulkner also uses the name 'Jiggs' for ironic effect: the reader of *Pylon* in 1935 would have been likely to associate the name with the leading character in the comic-strip *Bringing Up Father*, which was nationally syndicated at the time.[5] In the comic-strip, Jiggs is an Irish workman who becomes enormously wealthy but, contrary to the aspirations of his harridan of a wife, wishes to return to the simple life at the bottom of the social strata. Jiggs's footwear in *Pylon* constitutes a debased parallel to the spats habitually worn by his comic-strip counterpart, and the necessity of his keeping one eye shut throughout much of the latter part of the novel resembles the manner in which the comic-strip Jiggs was often pictured with one eye closed in astonishment at his wife's outrageous behavior. The comics are mentioned a number of times in *Pylon*, and in his story about fliers in the thirties Faulkner may have had particularly in mind the profusion of comic-strip fliers who appeared in the newspapers at the beginning of that decade: such comic-strips as *Tailspin Tommy, Skyroads, Flying to Fame,* and *Scorchy Smith* all appeared in the early thirties.[6]

The economic condition of the fliers in *Pylon* is, however, no laughing matter. The necessity of Roger's 'beating' the other fliers 'on the pylons' typifies their plight, and unlike the Jiggs of *Bringing Up Father*, who tries futilely to escape the tyranny of wealth, Faulkner's Jiggs desperately needs money. That, indeed, was his reason for joining the troupe; as he tells the bus driver, he stays away from his Kansas home because his wife took so much of his winnings that he (significantly enough, given the sorry state of his footwear in New Valois) 'couldnt even keep back enough to have [his] shoes halfsoled' (16). He goes on to explain that:

> 'Everytime I did a job her or the sheriff would catch the guy and get the money before I could tell him I was through; I would make a parachute jump and one of them would have the jack and be on the way back to town before I even pulled the ripcord.' (16)

Although Jiggs fails to note the correspondence, he later does to Jack Holmes precisely what he here accuses his wife and the sheriff of doing to him.

Jiggs's minor malfeasance in 'borrowing' Jack's earnings—for which he does, after all, attempt to make restitution—pales by comparison with the complete corruption of the ironically named Colonel Feinman, an amoral exploiter who imprints his foul signature on the entire community of New Valois. The airport's being named after him and its beacon flashing the first initial of his surname far and wide in Morse code illustrate the breadth of his influence, just as his position as chairman of the Sewage Board serves to suggest his personal corruption. His bloated physique, his bullying of Sales and Ord, his heavy-handed treatment of the fliers as a group, and the references to him as 'General Behindman'—all contribute to the impression of him as a sleazy opportunist and a trafficker in human flesh.

The presentation of Feinman, particularly in regard to his avarice and his exploitation of the fliers, was perhaps indebted to Dos Passos's 1928 play *Airways, Inc.*, in which the shady entrepreneur Jonathan P. Davis uses a *Wunderkind* of the air, Elmer Turner, to promote his company, 'All-American Airways, Inc.'[7] Davis cares as little about Elmer's safety as Feinman does about Roger's, and his slick lawyer, McGovern, resembles Feinman's 'eunuchmountebank' (223) secretary in his ability to gloss over the unsavory aspects of his employer's motives. Other features of *Airways, Inc.* also anticipate *Pylon*: the radical Walter's new hat seems as incongruous as Shumann's new homburg; the anonymous reporter in *Airways, Inc.* uses his identity as a member of the press to pass through police lines, as does the reporter in *Pylon*; the plane crashes of Elmer and Shumann both result from mechanical malfunctions; and the Professor's mandate in *Airways, Inc.* that 'we must make ourselves machines, machines of brass and nickel, we must turn our hearts into dynamos, our blood into electric current',[8] is, at least in the reporter's estimation, fulfilled by the fliers in *Pylon*.

Another Dos Passos work, the 1925 novel *Manhattan Transfer*, contains the story of Jimmy Herf, a reporter who, like the reporter in *Pylon*, is naive, drinks absinth—'like they make it in New Orleans', as one of the other characters remarks[9]—says 'Yare', as do many of the characters in the book and, perhaps most importantly, resembles *Pylon*'s reporter in his desire to quit newspaper work in order to write fiction. Portmanteau words, so characteristic of *Manhattan Transfer* and other Dos Passos works, also frequently appear in *Pylon*. The profusion of such words in *Pylon*—'slantshimmered' (7), 'painwebbed' (28), 'corpseglare' (41), 'lightlyclattering' (235), and so on—may have been deliberately implemented precisely in order to invoke Dos Passos and so to indicate the type of novel Faulkner was writing and to imply a standard against which it might be judged. The headlines in *Pylon* have been compared to the 'Newsreels' in Dos Passos's

U. S. A., but they seem much closer in form and function to those in *Manhattan Transfer*; in the latter, the fragmentary headlines are interwoven in the story itself—unlike the 'Newsreels' in *U. S. A.* which are separate from the narrative passages dealing directly with the characters—and anticipate those in *Pylon* in providing an indirect commentary both on the environment in which the novel is set and on the capacity for understanding of the reader of the paper. In *Pylon*, the reporter's drunkenly misreading a set of headlines in a 'loud declamatory voice' (109) signifies the inversion, or confusion, of traditional values typifying the fliers' relation to modern society—an inversion also suggested by the numerous references to characters flying upside down. It also characterizes the way in which the reporter generally misconstrues events, as well as his deficiencies in the relating of them.

Essential to our understanding of *Pylon* is the recognition that much of the presentation of the fliers is transmitted by—or filtered through the consciousness of—the reporter, whom Faulkner once referred to as 'the central character in the book'.[10] Thus, the turbulent prose of the narrative may be attributed to the reporter's agitated mental state after encountering the fliers. Like the Sutpen story in *Absalom, Absalom!*, the tale of the fliers is crucial not so much for its own sake as for the effect it produces on a perceiving intelligence. In this sense, *Pylon* is not so much about the ephemeral phenomenon which the fliers embody[11] as about the reporter's attempt to interpret that phenomenon, his struggle to extract meaning from and impose coherence on a series of activities and occurrences which, to borrow the narrative description of the reporter's own wallhanging, seem to him 'enigmatic of significance and inscrutable of purpose' (118). The reporter's aspiration to be a writer of fiction—which he avows to the newspaper editor, Hagood—combined with his attempt to 'read' the situation of the fliers affirms his function as both an artist-figure and a reader; hence, *Pylon*, like the other non-Yoknapatawpha novels, may be read as a fable of creativity.

The reporter in both of his roles bears an implicit responsibility to distinguish between fact and truth, a distinction which Faulkner himself drew time and again in interviews. For instance, in the interview with Jean Stein, he asserted that 'facts have very little connection with truth'.[12] And, in a rather combative interview with Betty Beale, Faulkner—interestingly enough considering the reporter's position in *Pylon*—commented upon the differing approaches of the creative writer and the journalist: 'I deal with people. You [journalists] deal with facts. Facts . . . bear no relation to truth'.[13] The distinction between fact and truth is highlighted in the novel by the contrast between, on the one hand, the newspaper headlines which appear sporadically throughout the text, and on the other, the chapter titles. In the narrative references to the headlines Faulkner emphasises the folly of trying to isolate a moment from the continuum of time through the mere reporting of facts:

> As the cage door clashed behind him, the editor himself reached down and lifted the facedown watch from the stack of papers, from that cryptic staccato crosssection of an instant crystallized and now dead two hours. (85)

And again:

> the fragile web of ink and paper, assertive, proclamative, profound and irrevocable if only in the sense of being profoundly and irrevocably unimportant . . . the dead instant's fruit of forty tons of machinery and an entire nation's antic delusion. (111—Faulkner's ellipsis)

Three of the chapter heads, by contrast, allude to works of literature which Faulkner held in high esteem: 'Tomorrow' and 'And Tomorrow' both derive from that soliloquy in *Macbeth* which provided the title for *The Sound and the Fury*; 'Lovesong of J. A. Prufrock' alludes, of course, to the poem by T. S. Eliot. The implied superiority of literature to journalism in *Pylon* reverberates in a review of Jimmy Collins's *Test Pilot* which Faulkner wrote for *American Mercury* in 1935, the year of *Pylon*'s publication: he felt that the non-autobiographical portions of Collins's novel smacked of 'sentimental journalese' because Collins had been 'a newspaper writer'.[14] Faulkner's distinction rests on his belief that literature transcends the time and place of composition, whereas 'news' is dead even before being written because the very nature of journalism causes reporting to be irrevocably *post facto*. Rather than murdering the moment by extracting it from time as newspapers do, literature captures the motion of life, revitalizing the moment by imbuing it, not with the ephemera of fact, but with the constancy of truth.

The reporter in *Pylon,* as the very designation 'the reporter' serves to suggest, fails to differentiate between fact and truth, and therefore does not individuate himself as a reader, an author, or, indeed, even as a reporter. Ultimately, as Faulkner suggested at Nagano, the reporter remains anonymous because he never earns a name:

> . . . my characters, luckily for me, name themselves. I never have to hunt for their names. Suddenly they tell me who they are. In the conception, quite often, but never very long after I have conceived that character, does he name himself. When he doesn't name himself, I never do. I have written about characters whose names I never did know. Because they didn't tell me. There was one in *Pylon,* for instance . . . he never did tell me who he was. . . . That was the reporter.[15]

Although the reporter has difficulty distinguishing between journalism and fiction, fact and truth, Faulkner assists the reader of *Pylon* in avoiding such a mistake by specifically emphasizing the novel's fabular aspects. The names of nearly all the characters suggest that *Pylon* be read as a fable: in addition to Holmes, Shumann and Jiggs, the names Leblanc, Legendre, Sales, Chance, Burnham and Bullitt all contribute to the fabular ambience of *Pylon*. The reporter's anonymity thus assumes added significance in suggesting his exclusion from this context of overtly literary significance. Faulkner's setting of the novel in New Valois, Franciana, rather than New Orleans, Louisiana, also highlights the primacy of fable in *Pylon*. A letter which Faulkner wrote to Harrison Smith in late December 1934 indicates that he was as adamant concerning the distinction between New Valois and New Orleans as he was elsewhere with regard to Jefferson and Oxford:

> And perhaps I had better mention this too. 'New Valois' is a thinly disguised (that is, someone will read the story and believe it to be) New Orleans . . . . But the incidents in Pylon are all fiction and Feinman is fiction so far as I know . . . . the story and incidents and the characters as they perform in the story are all fictional.[16]

The chapter heads, the numerous references to drama and stage properties (in particular, the theater curtain which divides the reporter's room in half and thus separates him from the lovemaking of the fliers), the allusions to writers such as Eliot and Dos Passos, and the explicit mention of 'Lewises . . . Hemingways . . . Tchekovs . . . [and] even Nobel Prize fiction' (50)—all add to the explicitly literary context in which Faulkner couches the story of the reporter. The various descriptions of him also teem with literary references and allusions: for example, when he and Shumann visit Ord's home, the reporter brings 'into the house, the room, that atmosphere of a fifteenth century Florentine stage scene—an evening call with formal courteous words in the mouth and naked rapiers under the cloaks' (167–68). When speaking with Jiggs after Roger's death, the reporter casts himself in the role of an actor in a 'good orthodox Italian tragedy' in which, appropriately enough, 'one Florentine falls in love with another Florentine's wife' (279). Jiggs time and again refers to the reporter as 'Lazarus', a designation which not only recalls the biblical story of the resurrection of Lazarus (perhaps, given the economic context of *Pylon*, the parable of Lazarus and Dives as well), but also contains an allusion to the passage in 'The Love Song of J. Alfred Prufrock' in which Prufrock envisions himself as 'Lazarus, come from the dead,/ Come back to tell you all, I shall tell you all'[17]—the point presumably being that Prufrock and the reporter are equally incapable of imparting anything of significance to the reader except through implication.

The reporter's insufficiencies in comprehending the dimensions of the drama which unfolds before him account in part for the emphasis laid upon his spectral qualities, the sheer insubstantiality of his physical appearance. The first time the reporter is mentioned in *Pylon* he is described as looking like 'something which had apparently crept from a doctor's cupboard and, in the snatched garments of an etherised patient in a charity ward, escaped into the living world' (20). This description should not only alert readers to the reporter's limitations but, with its rather explicit allusion to the opening lines of 'Prufrock', should also prepare them for the numerous allusions to other literary works and figures associated, explicitly or implicitly, with the reporter. As Millgate observes, the reporter is 'many-fathered',[18] and this could apply not only to his mother's insatiable appetite for marriage but also to his literary forebears. For example, he shares certain affinities with Irving's Ichabod Crane, who is mentioned in *The Hamlet* and who, like the reporter, is ungainly in appearance, has literary aspirations, and attempts to win his way into the good graces of a mother through her child. Another predecessor of the reporter's seems to be St Christopher, who is regularly depicted as fording a river with the Christ-child on his shoulder: the reporter, described at one point as the 'patron (even if no guardian) saint of all waifs' (183), often carries Jackie on his shoulder as he threads his way through the crowds or fords the 'Lethe' (80) of Grandlieu Street. The full irony of the association becomes apparent when one recalls that anyone who looks on an image of St Christopher is said to be protected from death that day, that he reputedly guards against death by water, and that in the early twentieth century he became the patron saint of motorists and aviators.[19]

A more explicit allusion appears in the description of the reporter as leaning over Hagood's desk like an eager skeleton, with 'that air of worn and dreamy fury which Don Quixote must have had' (49), a resemblance confirmed by the reporter's often envisioning what is not there and seldom seeing what is. In a sense, his problem seems the reverse of Quixote's in that Cervantes's mad knight assumes fiction to be fact, while the reporter mistakes fact for fiction; nevertheless the results remain much the same in that both are self-deluded. The properties of the so-called 'absinth' which the reporter buys are as illusory as those of the 'balsam' which Quixote prepares, and the reporter's vomiting fails to dispel his illusion about the alcohol just as Quixote's vomiting merely reinforces his belief in the miraculous potency of the 'medicine' he ingests. Quixote, dubbed by Sancho the 'Knight of the Sorrowful Countenance', is obviously unsuitable as a chivalric knight in the mold of his hero, Amadis de Gaul; yet, his physical condition notwithstanding, he pursues adventure and invents quests in the hope of emulating the fictional personages he so admires. Similarly, although poorly suited for mere survival, much less flying, the reporter attaches himself to the fliers in the vain hope of being accepted by them. Despite his sexual designs on Laverne, his dedication to her recalls Quixote's feelings towards 'Dulcinea del Toboso', and his attitude regarding the fliers as a group seems equally quixotic: at least part of the time he views them as modern-day knights of the air who, somewhat akin to Quixote's fictional heroes, become habituated to dispensing with food and sleep in preparation for mounting their silver chargers and soaring into the glory of competitive daring.

This, however, is only one pole of the reporter's perspective, for at other times he sees the fliers as mere extensions of the planes they fly and service. His self-perpetuated illusions concerning the fliers cause him to oscillate radically between two attitudes, one romantic, the other cynical, and each leads to a distorted perspective on the 'characters' whom he re-presents to Hagood and, indeed, to the reader. When viewing the fliers romantically, the reporter uses the plural personal pronoun 'we', indicative of an inordinate sympathy with—and involvement in—their predicament; when considering them cynically, he uses 'they', suggestive of his distancing himself from their behavior or even of an antipathy towards it. The reporter's inadequacies as a narrator are captured in Holmes's comment, 'Maybe he cant even read his own writing' (82), just as his bifurcated attitude towards the fliers renders the 'fourth reporter's' remark in the final chapter concerning 'the flying Jekyll and Hyde brother' (290) directly applicable to the reporter himself.

A number of commentators on the novel have found fault with Faulkner for the ambivalent tone of *Pylon*, suggesting that he was unable to reconcile his admiration for the fliers with his presentation of them as examples of the dehumanizing effects of the machine age. The 'ambivalence' of tone, however, rests not with Faulkner but with the controlling consciousness in the novel, the reporter. Whereas Faulkner presumably held both views of the fliers in suspension, the reporter repeatedly shifts completely from one polarized judgment of them to the other. Just prior to Shumann's crash, for instance, he refers to the fliers as non-human machines, despite his having witnessed their human qualities for three days. The narrative insertion in the midst of the reporter's reverie makes clear that this inconsistency belongs to the reporter rather than to Faulkner:

> 'That's it,' he thought quietly, with that faint quiet grimace almost like smiling; 'they aint human. It aint adultery; you cant anymore imagine two of them making love than you can two of them airplanes back in the corner of the hangar, coupled.' With one hand he supported the boy on his shoulder, feeling through the harsh khaki the young brief living flesh. 'Yair; cut him and it's cylinder oil; dissect him and it aint bones: it's little rockerarms and connecting rods. . . .' (231—Faulkner's ellipsis)

Jackie's physical presence proves that the fliers do make love and his 'young brief living flesh' (not to mention the death of Roger which follows shortly after the above statement) belies the reporter's assertion that his parents are some type of twentieth-century machine. The reporter's refrain 'they aint human' which appears in this passage gives clear evidence of his failure in perspective and may seem even more damning in light of the fact that Faulkner would later put precisely the same phrase in the mouth of the notoriously narrow-minded deputy in 'Pantaloon in Black' as an expression of the deputy's gross misconception of the motivations and activities of Rider and of blacks in general.[20] A narrative comment concerning the reporter in *Pylon* when hung-over indirectly pinpoints his problem in developing two mutually exclusive interpretations of the fliers' activities: 'indeed, the very fact of his insistence to himself should have been intimation enough that things were not all right' (108).

Largely because of his divided attitude, the reporter remains obsessed with the fliers. In this absorption, he resembles a typical Faulknerian 'demon-driven' writer, but his involvement with his 'characters' goes beyond the bounds of artistic control and leads to his projecting onto the fliers his own idiosyncrasies, deficiencies, aspirations, and even physical habits. His contention that they do not need money, sleep, or food would be more properly applied to himself: if he wants money, he borrows it with ease; he gets almost no sleep during the course of the novel; and he must remind himself to eat, as if it were a matter of will and memory rather than of physical necessity.

In the reporter's opinion, one of the most appealing aspects of the lives of the fliers is their apparent capacity to escape the mundanity of day-to-day existence; he feels that they live in an eternal present, that for them 'tomorrow and tomorrow do not count because that will be at the airfield' (62). As he tells Shumann, he wishes to join the troupe not only to remain close to Laverne, but also to evade the monotony of a life circumscribed by the regimentation of time:

> 'Because it's thinking about the day after tomorrow and the day after that and after that and me smelling the same burnt coffee and dead shrimp and oysters and waiting for the same light to change, like me and the red light worked on the same clock so I could cross and get home and go to bed so I could get up and

start smelling the coffee and fish and waiting for the light to change again.' (176)

The 'tomorrow and tomorrow and tomorrow' references in *Pylon* anticipate Temple Drake's distress in *Requiem for a Nun* over the seemingly interminable procession of the days ahead—an anxiety not unlike that of the reporter—and Laverne resembles Temple in being strong and yet wanting a stable domestic situation. The 'tomorrow' references also evoke the shade of Quentin Compson who appears as the central character in *Absalom, Absalom!*, the novel upon which Faulkner had been working before setting it aside to write *Pylon* and who, like Shumann in *Pylon*, evades time only through his death by water. It becomes increasingly evident as *Pylon* progresses that although the fliers may have (to refer to Faulkner's remarks on barnstormers at the University of Virginia) 'escaped the compulsion of accepting a past',[21] this 'escape' leads simply to a repetition of former follies: Jiggs remains in no financial position to afford other than 'halfsoled' shoes; Laverne must again endure the agony of loss and bereavement, first with Roger and then with Jackie; and Roger's earlier plane crashes, one of which occurs while rescuing Laverne from a perilous situation, presage his final crash into the lake.

Hence, the reporter's desire to escape time through his association with the fliers is misguided, a manifestation of that willed innocence and naiveté he uses to support his illusions until they collapse as a result of Roger's death. The reporter's almost catatonic state following the crash indicates the profound effect which both it and Laverne's rejection have had upon him. In the penultimate chapter, the trauma occasioned by Roger's death seems to have had a positive outcome, for the reporter is apparently at last prepared to adopt a quintessentially Faulknerian attitude: 'tomorrow and tomorrow and tomorrow; not only not to hope, not even to wait: just to endure' (284).

It is fitting that the Mardi Gras festivities should end on the day after Roger's death,[22] for throughout *Pylon* the Mardi Gras celebration in New Valois not only heightens by contrast the plight of the fliers but serves to reflect the reporter's mental state: his wild and aberrant attitudes and behavior correspond to the bizarre and chaotic aspects of the festival, and his cadaver-like appearance matches the costumes worn by the revellers. His physical condition makes him appear to be just one more grotesque in a city full of freaks, and it is therefore appropriate that he was born on April Fools' Day. Given the close correlation between the celebration in the city and the reporter's extreme perspectives, the empty streets on the day after Roger dies may be seen to parallel the reporter's numbed and chastened faculties. The vision which leads the reporter to his near acceptance of the 'ten thousand inescapable mornings' (284) he faces after the departure of Laverne and Holmes involves his recognition of the ephemerality intrinsic to both the celebration and his own relationship with the fliers. Consequently, he comes to realize that he cannot elude the venality and mundanity which characterizes everyday life in New Valois:

> By looking back he could still see the city, the glare of it, no further away; if he were moving, regardless at what terrific speed and in what loneliness, so was it, paralleling him. He was not escaping it; symbolic and encompassing it outlay all gasolinespanned distances and all clock- or sun-stipulated destinations. It would be there—the eternal smell of the coffee the sugar the hemp. (283–84)

The reporter's attitude in the final chapter of *Pylon*, however, demonstrates that he has failed to retain the insight achieved during this apparent epiphany. His perspective becomes fragmented once again, and his uncharacteristic silence throughout the opening pages of 'The Scavengers' may result from the equally anonymous other reporters' giving voice to those opposing attitudes between which he has himself oscillated. The 'first reporter' takes a predominantly cynical view of the activities of the fliers, while the 'second reporter' advocates a primarily romantic interpretation; since each adopts an extreme position, neither is entirely accurate in his assessment of the actions of Holmes and Laverne after Shumann's death. That the two reporters may be read as personified projections of the contradictions within the reporter's mind is suggested by the fact that, although apparently oblivious to their prattle, he nevertheless suddenly leaves to investigate the first reporter's assertion that Laverne and Holmes intend to leave Jackie with Roger's parents.

The two reporters in 'The Scavengers' construct divergent and imperfect 'readings' of the story of the fliers: each interpretation contains aspects of truth, but a complete and judicious reading would ultimately have to include elements from each account. The two obituaries which the reporter writes indicate that he is finally unequal to constructing such a reading: the first is hopelessly romantic, wallowing in a mire of sophomoric sentimentality; the second is vitriolic, seething with a bitter cynicism. The description of the reporter as he sits at the typewriter preparing to compose his first obituary intimates that the forthcoming attempt to produce even the 'beginning of literature' (314) will be futile. The alcohol that the reporter drinks, which 'tasted, felt, like so much dead icy water, cold and heavy and lifeless in his stomach' (301–2), serves as anaesthetic rather than inspiration and, not unlike the resulting prose, it is 'sluggish and dead' (302). The reporter's inability to 'feel his fingers on the keys' (302) of the typewriter signifies his lack of real sensitivity regarding his material.

Whereas the reporter's two obituaries present negative examples of the potential results of the creative process, the narrative episode involving Laverne's meeting with Dr Shumann provides an authentic literary product. The abruptness of the transition from the description of the reporter seated at the typewriter beginning his first obituary to the story of Laverne, Jackie and Dr Shumann suggests that the latter episode represents not simply a continuation of the saga of the fliers but a possible result of the process of composition itself, an exemplification of the type of literature which the reporter should be trying to create—a treatment of life in all its complexity and ambiguity, rather than a brooding upon death from one or the other of two extreme and oversimplified perspectives. The reporter has most of the material necessary to formulate such a story: for example, he knows that Laverne, Holmes and Jackie are bound for Myron, Ohio, and that Dr Shumann is a relatively poor small-town doctor who apparently had to place a mortgage on his farm to cover Roger's debts. The other details in the story the reporter could supply from his imagination; he has had, after all, a type of rudimentary instruction in the methods of imaginative re-creation in those conversations with Jiggs in which the latter fleshed out the few facts he possessed concerning Roger and Laverne's past.

One crucial fact of which the reporter remains unaware is Laverne's pregnancy; yet his failing to envision such a possibility only further emphasises his imaginative deficiencies. This is also a failure of the heart in that he refuses to view Laverne's situation sympathetically, even to the extent of giving her the benefit of the doubt with regard to her motives for leaving Jackie with Dr Shumann—a failure comparable to the doctor's facile acceptance of his wife's innuendo concerning the source of the money found in the toy plane.[23] Affinities between Dr Shumann and the reporter are implied elsewhere in the novel: both the soldier at the airport and Jiggs address the reporter as 'doc', the latter doing so four times just shortly after the reporter learns that Laverne was taking Jackie to Dr Shumann's (296–97), and the doctor resembles the reporter not only in his physical 'spareness' (313) but also in his manner of speaking in a 'curious loud wild rushing manner' (306). Like the attenuated narrator in Eliot's 'Gerontion', Dr Shumann is an 'old man in a draughty house' and his remark that he and his wife would be more comfortable about accepting Jackie 'If we just had a sign' (310) echoes those in 'Gerontion' who insist 'We would see a sign'.[24] The 'sign' which Dr Shumann believes that he eventually discerns in all probability results, like so many of the reporter's deductions, from self delusion, although the reader can never be sure of this. It is, however, certain that unlike the lifeless obituaries which the reporter writes, the story of Laverne's meeting with Dr Shumann—and for that matter the story of the reporter himself as related by Faulkner—is an authentic tale of the human heart in conflict with itself.

The reporter's postscript to Hagood which follows the second version of the obituary demonstrates that he has made no permanent progress since he first encountered the fliers:

> *I guess this is what you want you bastard and now I am going down to Amboise st. and get drunk a while and if you dont know where Amboise st. is ask your son to tell you and if you dont know what drunk is come down there and look at me and when you come bring some jack because I am on a credit* (315)

Not only does the reporter again immerse himself in the tawdry world of illusion where immediate sensation replaces genuine feeling, but the lack of punctuation in the postscript and its abrupt truncation suggests the urgency with which he returns to his ephemeral pastimes. The incompleteness of the novel's final sentence also suggests that *Pylon* itself remains unfinished—as indeed it does if we expect a conclusion to resolve all the problems raised in the text—and that Faulkner invites the reader to complete it. He thus ensures that his novel constitutes more than a 'dead instant' removed from the continuum of time. After completing a first reading of *Pylon*, one must continue to ponder it, to examine it, to wrestle with it, in order to arrive at some reasonable approximation of its meaning. In this respect *Pylon* anticipates *Absalom, Absalom!*: as with the narrators in *Absalom*, Faulkner's use of an unreliable center of consciousness in *Pylon* guarantees that the interaction between the reader and the text will be an ongoing, dynamic process—that the reader will attempt again and again to piece together yet another version of the story, to construct that 'fourteenth image of [the] blackbird' which may contain the work's essential meaning.[25]

As in *Absalom, Absalom!*, Faulkner's primary concern in *Pylon* involves not so much the actions of the nominal subjects of the story as the narrative processes and prejudices which foster equally unsatisfactory interpretations. The narrative modes of both *Absalom* and *Pylon* not only reveal the salient aspects of the interpreting consciousness but also draw the reader inexorably into the process of interpretation and, indeed, of fictional representation. Just as Shreve McCannon, according to the genealogy appended to *Absalom*, steps out of the novel and is 'now' a practising surgeon in Edmonton, Alberta, so, in a sense, must the reader enter into both *Pylon* and *Absalom* as a character, emulating the attempts of the other characters to arrive at a more comprehensive understanding of the fable within and engaging in a joint effort along with those characters to grasp meanings which elude an immediate apprehension.

The reader of *Pylon* thus assumes a position analogous to that of the copyboy who finds the fragments of the reporter's first obituary scattered on the floor or dropped in the wastebasket by the reporter's desk:

> He gathered up from the floor all the sheets, whole and in fragments, emptied the wastebasket and, sitting at the reporter's desk he began to sort them, discarding and fitting and resorting at the last to paste; then, his eyes big with excitement and exultation and then downright triumph, he regarded what he had salvaged and restored to order and coherence—the sentences and paragraphs which he believed to be not only news but the beginning of literature. (314)

The copyboy's method of discarding, fitting, and even resorting to paste closely approximates what Faulkner himself did with his own manuscripts at various stages in the genesis of both *Pylon* and *Absalom, Absalom!*.[26] Hence, the dynamic interaction between the reader and the text in both novels mirrors not only the search in which the protagonists engage but part of the process of composition as well, as seems entirely appropriate to two novels in which the reader must actively participate in the re-creation of the work in order to appreciate its full complexity. This deliberate extension of the creative process in *Pylon* may induce in the reader a feeling like that of the copyboy once he has assembled the inchoate information he has received from the reporter into a coherent form: 'O Jesus,' he whispered. 'Maybe Hagood will let me finish it!' (314). Nonetheless, although the copyboy may be 'bright' and 'ambitious' (314), his exaltation of the 'sentimental journalese' produced by the reporter indicates that he is not particularly skilled as a reader and, presumably, still less so as a writer.

Although the copyboy's 'becoming a more complete vassal to surprise than ever' (314) when he sees the second obituary seems appropriate enough, this cynical obituary should come as no surprise to the reader. Throughout *Pylon* the reporter has in effect used the same material to tell two stories, just as he composes two radically different obituaries on a single flier, and it is not too much to say that this constant shifting from one excessive attitude to the other makes it possible to read *Pylon* either as a tragedy or as a comedy. Although its tragic aspects may dominate, the novel clearly incorporates comedy as well—a combination which characterizes much of Faulkner's work. The reporter himself comments to Jiggs on the mixture of the tragic and the comic in his interaction with the fliers:

> 'It started out to be a tragedy. A good orthodox Italian tragedy. You know: one Florentine falls in love with another Florentine's wife . . . and so just as the curtain falls on the third act the Florentine and the wife crawl down the fire escape . . . . But it went wrong. When he come climbing up to the window to tell her the horses was ready, she refused to speak to him. It turned into a comedy, see?' (279)[27]

Characteristically, the reporter sees tragedy and comedy as mutually exclusive, but the immediately juxtaposed description of his mingled tears and laughter, anticipatory of the Norman's reaction in the conclusion of *A Fable*, illustrates the extent to which in *Pylon* the two modes persistently intertwine.

A remark that Faulkner made concerning the use of humor in his novels pertains to the tragicomic characteristics of *Pylon*:

> there's not too fine a distinction between humor and tragedy, that even tragedy is in a way walking a tightrope between the ridiculous—between the bizarre and the terrible . . . . That [the writer] will use humor, tragedy, just as he uses violence. They are tools, but an [sic] ineradicable parts of life, that humor is.[28]

Although in these comments Faulkner is speaking of humor rather than of comedy, *Pylon* demonstrates that he considered both tragedy and comedy 'ineradicable parts' of life, simultaneously inhering in any human situation. The numerous references to stage comedy, comics, vaudeville, and even the reporter's appearance counterbalance the tragic elements in *Pylon* and thereby indicate the co-existence of polarities. The reporter's problem therefore is not so much that he fails to synthesize the opposed aspects of the fliers' story as that he neglects to hold them in suspension. In moving from one pole to the other he ignores the possibility that both positions may in one way or another be valid, his perspective remaining invariably exclusive and simplistic.

Although *Pylon may* be construed either as a tragedy or as a comedy, it should not be analyzed solely in terms of either, for much of the meaning of the work lies in the tension created by their juxtaposition in the story which the reporter is so inept at understanding and conveying. Another such juxtaposition lies in the fact that nearly every significant action taken by the characters contains elements of both right and wrong: the money which Jiggs takes to buy the boots is owed to him but his spending the money forces the fliers to depend on the reporter for necessities; the reporter's arranging for Shumann and himself to buy the plane appears to be the answer to the fliers' dilemma but instead results in Shumann's death; Shumann's flying the plane in the Trophy race highlights both his selfless bravery and his foolhardiness; Laverne feels compelled by economic considerations to leave Jackie with Dr Shumann, but the prospects for the boy's future with the eccentric doctor and his suspicious wife are bleak; the construction of the airport provides the citizens of New Valois with a valuable addition to the community but becomes at the same time a monstrosity of self-aggrandizement for Feinman. The reporter's—and the reader's—difficulty in determining the appropriate moral construction to apply to a particular character's actions is compounded in *Absalom, Absalom!*, whose narrators can never even be sure of precisely which putative actions were in fact performed by the subjects in the Sutpen story.

The multivalence of interpretation in *Pylon* anticipates that in *Absalom* and transforms what might otherwise be a single story into two stories—stories which must first be distinguished and then held in suspension by the reader in order to come to terms with the novel as a whole. In *Pylon*, the reporter uses the same material to present two radically different stories; in the following non-Yoknapatawpha novel, *The Wild Palms*, Faulkner himself would use two completely divergent tales—one tragic and one comic—to tell a single story. As with *Pylon*, as with all of the non-Yoknapatawpha novels, that story too constitutes a fable of creativity.

5

The Wild Palms

The Wild Palms is generally considered to be as puzzling as it is disturbing. The typical critical reaction when the novel first appeared in 1939 expressed consternation and confusion: not surprisingly, perhaps, many reviewers castigated Faulkner for yoking together two such seemingly disparate narratives; others, although more sympathetic to his resolute experimentalism, remained oblivious to the links between the two sections.[1] This misunderstanding of the structure of the book is reflected in its publishing history: the New American Library published the work as two separate novels in 1948; then in 1954 they placed both 'Wild Palms' and 'Old Man' in one volume but separated the sections into discrete units rather than alternating chapters, attempting perhaps to appeal to bargain-hunters by stating on the paper cover that the contents comprised 'Two complete novels originally published in one volume, entitled *The Wild Palms*'. In 1946, *The Portable Faulkner* contained 'Old Man' without 'Wild Palms'; and in 1950, the Modern Library first published that literary land-mine still available in the Vintage edition: *Three Famous Short Novels: Spotted Horses, Old Man, The Bear*.

Recent commentary, such as McHaney's *William Faulkner's 'The Wild Palms': A Study*, has helped to elucidate the numerous parallels and juxtapositions which emerge when one accepts *The Wild Palms* as the single novel Faulkner intended it to be, thereby counteracting that misconception of the novel as a gratuitous fusion of two essentially autonomous stories. It remains true, however, that on a first reading the radical juxtaposition of the stories produces surprise, mystification, even shock. As Grimwood puts it, 'with every shift from one chapter to the next, the reader must repeal his suspension of disbelief and rejustify the act of reading in which he is engaged'.[2] The impact of the transition from 'Wild Palms' to 'Old Man', the stark immediacy of this departure from traditional narrative, thereby compels the reader to search for meanings and correspondences not immediately apparent. The reader's reaction as he begins the second chapter may well resemble that of the tall convict as he is swept into the apparent chaos of the flood: as with *Pylon*, the reader of *The Wild Palms* is obligated to embark upon an investigation strikingly similar to that in which the characters themselves are involved.

It is almost as if *The Wild Palms* were a fictional primer for reader-response analysis: the structure of the novel undermines traditional concepts of narrative and plot and insists upon a recognition of the reader as a key component in the juncture of the two stories. If, that is, the two stories *should* be allied in the reader's mind. At one point in the pre-publication stages of the work Faulkner had both stories take place in 1927[3]; his decision to separate them by ten years attests to his desire to emphasise their disjunction. He habitually referred to 'Old Man' as the 'antithesis' of 'Wild Palms', thus further underscoring their opposition, and one can even say that in a sense the tension created by that opposition constitutes much of the meaning of the novel.

The relationship between 'Wild Palms' and 'Old Man' can be approached in terms of an almost infinite range of antitheses, and although these never prove to be entirely precise or definitive they do provide avenues of approach to this difficult text. For example, the two stories may be read as a masque and an antimasque, as a tragedy and a comedy, or even as Faulkner's version of Melville's 'The Paradise of Bachelors and the Tartarus of Maids'. Still another method of entering into the complexities of *The Wild Palms* is to read it as a fictional representation of two mutually exclusive modes of dealing with heartbreak: Harry accepts the grief engendered by his first love affair and consequently, as is made clear at the end of 'Wild Palms', extracts meaning and life from the tragedy; the convict, on the other hand, denies the pain wrought by his first love's rejecting him for another, and so learns nothing from the relationship.

In 1952 Faulkner wrote to Joan Williams that while working on *A Fable* he suddenly 'remembered how [he] wrote THE WILD PALMS in order to try to stave off what [he] thought was heartbreak'[4]—presumably a reference to what appeared in the late thirties to be the end of his relationship with Meta Carpenter. In subjecting himself to this work-cure Faulkner adhered to an axiom postulated by Julius in *Mosquitoes*, that earlier Faulkner novel apparently also written to 'stave off' heartbreak: 'Lucky he who believes that his heart is broken: he can immediately write a book

. . . . you don't commit suicide when you are disappointed in love. You write a book' (228). Indeed, it is possible to read the very different responses to heartbreak of the convict and Harry as reflecting either the two choices which Faulkner faced after the end of each affair or the contrast between his inclination as a young man in 1927 and his more mature response ten years later.

There are numerous examples of correspondences between the two novels: the peregrinations of both couples in *The Wild Palms,* for instance, have much in common with Patricia and David's excursion in *Mosquitoes;* the function of McCord and the plump convict as deflators of grandiose or misdirected sentiments approximates that of Julius and Eva; and Harry's remark about '*the people in the books inventing and reading about us*'[5] combines with other references to fictional characterization in *The Wild Palms* to establish much the same atmosphere of metafiction as that developed during those discussions aboard the *Nausikaa* when the members of the yachting party indirectly discuss their own validity as characters. As McHaney observes, the dynamiting of the levee in 'Old Man' occurs on 29 April 1927, and it seems more than coincidence that the publication date of *Mosquitoes* was 30 April 1927.[6]

That *The Wild Palms* shares so many affinities with *Mosquitoes* may suggest that in the later novel Faulkner quite consciously reworks the concerns of the apprenticeship book from a more sophisticated perspective. In *Mosquitoes,* as we have seen, art constitutes a major concern both of the characters in the novel and of the novel itself. In *The Wild Palms* Faulkner conducts a less obtrusive but nonetheless comparable exploration into the meaning of art and the functions and obligations of both artist and reader. The abundant allusions to other literary works in *The Wild Palms* signal the centrality of literature itself to the thematic concerns of the novel and it is notable that while the most prominent allusions in 'Old Man' generally relate to writers of works already established as classics, those in 'Wild Palms' primarily concern Faulkner's contemporaries. This difference can be directly associated with the distinction which Faulkner drew between his 'masters' and his 'contemporaries',[7] and suggests another factor in Faulkner's decision to separate the two stories. 'Old Man' in many instances, such as the encounter with the steamboat on the Mississippi, recalls *The Adventures of Huckleberry Finn,* while 'Wild Palms' contains many allusions to *A Farewell to Arms* and other works by Hemingway, as well as McCord's rather Joycean reference to 'hemingwaves' (97). These quite deliberate correspondences compel the reader's consideration. Faulkner stated on a number of occasions that he considered Mark Twain to be the 'father' of American literature,[8] and at the time *The Wild Palms* was being written Hemingway was the most famous contemporary American novelist. Through his sundry allusions to such well-known American authors Faulkner appears to have been suggesting that the best work of both his 'masters' and his 'contemporaries' might and should be used as a standard for the evaluation of his own literary achievement.

Although 'Old Man' is set in 1927, the allusions to such works as the *Odyssey*, the Bible, and *Huckleberry Finn*, when combined with the general description of the circumstances of the convict's voyage and struggle for survival, invoke a time-span ranging from the primeval to the twentieth century. The first sentence of 'Old Man'—'Once (it was in Mississippi, in May, in the flood year 1927) there were two convicts' (23)—announces to the reader through its mixture of the fairy-tale and naturalistic modes both the fabular nature of the ensuing story and the kind of narrative detail by which that fable will unfold. 'Old Man' consequently serves as a fabular literary backdrop or context for 'Wild Palms', even though that is in one sense precisely the opposite of what one might expect. 'Wild Palms', after all, is deliberately divorced from Faulkner's fictional county, while 'Old Man' bears at least a tangential relation to Yoknapatawpha—its action originates and concludes in Mississippi, and in the map which Faulkner provided for *The Portable Faulkner* (1946) he indicated that the tall convict was born in the hill country surrounding Frenchman's Bend—and it is, in general, the non-Yoknapatawpha novels which provide allusive literary and overtly fabular contexts for the Yoknapatawpha fiction, rather than the other way round. It is tempting to speculate that this provides one of the reasons why Faulkner did not set the central action of 'Old Man' specifically in Yoknapatawpha, although another, more pragmatic, reason could well be that he did not want 'Old Man' to take precedence over 'Wild Palms': in his public comments on *The Wild Palms*, he time and again insisted on the primacy of the story of Harry and Charlotte.[9] Despite this inversion of the characteristic functions of the two settings in *The Wild Palms*, the neccessity for reading the text as a unified novel pertains directly to our reading of Faulkner's work as a whole.

The connections between the Yoknapatawpha and the non-Yoknapatawpha texts must be made by the reader of the canon independent of direct authorial correlation—very much the kind of procedure which the reader must adopt in order to appreciate *The Wild Palms* as a single, unified text.

Upon achieving that recognition of the correspondences and oppositions which characterize the relations between 'Wild Palms' and 'Old Man', it becomes clear that the two stories actually present a single fable dealing with, among other things, art and the artist. All three of the major characters in the novel—Charlotte, Harry, and even the tall convict—in some sense come to represent artist-figures or at least embodiments of impulses within the artist. And one of the central oppositions among these characters involves the conflict between the artist's ambition for inspired expression and the need to formulate that expression within a cogent structure. Harry and Charlotte attempt to dispense with order, with convention, with structure, and fail in that attempt; and just as they become unsuccessful anarchists, so the tall convict emerges as a frustrated authoritarian, for he believes in order for its own sake and futilely tries to impose it on the flood, a force which by its very nature derides his puny attempts to secure stability. The attitudes of the major characters are as extreme as the environs they come to inhabit. The convict advocates pattern without meaning; Charlotte is a priestess of meaning without pattern; and only Harry, at the end of 'Wild Palms', combines pattern and meaning and thereby grasps the possibility of an authentic, inclusive perspective.

This opposition between the rebellion against an externally imposed, confining structure and the necessity for order finds a correlation in the relentless experimentalism of Faulkner's own writing. The opulent prose of his 'high rhetorical' style deliberately disregards conventions of grammar, sentence structure, and traditional novelistic technique so that the meaning in the prose may strike the reader with maximum impact; his restless search for the precise structure best capable of expressing the essence of each novel evinces his recognition of the value of—and the necessity for—an order which illuminates, rather than restricts, meaning. Samuel Beckett, in his study of Proust, sums up a similar opposition in a phrase which Faulkner himself might have appreciated: 'The whisky bears a grudge against the decanter'.[10] To apply this expression to the characters in *The Wild Palms*, one might say that Charlotte wants only the whisky, the fire, the passion, but cannot retain it because she smashes the decanter in the attempt to get to it; the tall convict desires, and receives, only the decanter, emptied of the fuel for passion; while Harry at the end of 'Wild Palms' decides (to paraphrase Faulkner in his interview with Jean Stein) that, since he cannot have the (bourbon) whisky, between Scotch and nothing he will take Scotch—but he also recognizes the need for the jug.[11]

A variation on this opposition and resolution appears in the respective attitudes of the convict, Charlotte and Harry towards language. The convict initially accepts language as presence, fiction as reality, but becomes disenchanted when confronted with the inexorable difference between word and origin, ultimately assuming—as does Gordon in *Mosquitoes*—that the arbitrary value of verbal signs renders language unreliable and largely irrelevant in day-to-day life. The convict becomes enraged when life fails to accord with the formulae he extracts from literature and so for the most part rejects language as untrustworthy. Charlotte, on the other hand, tries to shape life to coincide with a romantic perspective chiefly fomented by the reading she has done, the denial of responsibility underlying her insistence on the abortion paralleling her denial of the insufficiency of language as the sole determinant of reality. Harry's approach to language moves from one perspective to the other, at one time debasing words into 'moron's pap' (122), at another, as his conversations with McCord demonstrate, accepting language as the foundation of a romantic panacea. Harry's alternation of attitudes, however, indicates a dissatisfaction with each of these equally invalid perspectives and manifests his persistent attempts to use language as a tool in understanding, discovering, and defining truth. Indeed, his epiphany at the conclusion of 'Wild Palms' depends specifically upon his ability to 'think it into words' (323). Cognizant of the inability of language to recapture or reconstitute presence, Harry nonetheless comes to a recognition of the necessity of articulating grief, an act which serves to combat the oblivion to which time would otherwise consign all human action and emotion. The implicit correlation of memory, recognition and articulation in Harry's epiphany reflects Faulkner's assertion that writing provides a means of saying 'no' to death, that one uses words to remember, recognize and relate—even if only to oneself—the significance immanent in human affairs.

The typescript for *The Wild Palms* indicates that Faulkner had at one time considered 'Rittlemeyer' as a possible surname for Charlotte, but eventually decided on 'Rittenmeyer',[12] a name which by virtue of its German cognates signifies her position as an artist-figure. Appropriately enough, Harry meets her at a gathering of New Orleans bohemians. She lies to Harry when they first meet, telling him that she is a painter when in fact she is a sculptress of sorts, and although she later emends this statement, the initial lie illustrates the manner in which she deludes others and, more importantly, herself throughout 'Wild Palms'. She insists on the purity of passion and affects disdain for social convention, yet her refusal to have sexual relations in the hotel room or in the company of the aptly named Buckners reveals that she remains tightly bound by bourgeois attitudes and mores. She likewise intimates to Harry that she wants to isolate their love out of the 'loud world', but she is nonetheless responsible for jamming it in with others in Chicago; and despite her apparent rejection of traditional male-female roles, during that same interlude in Chicago she plays the part of the happy homemaker. In theory, her desire to burn with the intensity of a hard gem-like flame compels admiration, but it becomes apparent to the reader, if not to Harry, that much of her posturing in this respect remains just that: an act in which the scenes may change but the actress herself is consistently self-deceived. The play—or perhaps movie (given the influence of the work Faulkner had been doing in Hollywood prior to writing *The Wild Palms*)—in which Charlotte casts herself in a starring role becomes a tragedy precisely because she remains so wilfully blind to her own deficiencies. For example, she never admits to herself that her obsessive desire for intense passion stems from her fear of the deadening of love experienced in her relationship with her husband, an erosion of emotion which she apparently attributes to the burden of children and the stagnancy of familiar surroundings.

While Charlotte's desire to escape the responsibilities of family routine mandates her and Harry's departure from New Orleans, her inability to obtain a divorce from her husband suggests the superficiality of her attempt to evade responsibility by fleeing from it. The departure also provides one of the many occurrences in the novel which suggest that Charlotte is not only an actress but a kind of director as well: she devises and directs scenarios dedicated to her own ardently-held beliefs. She feels that in doing so she pays obeisance to the great god Passion, but in effect she merely betrays her fear and the sterility which accompanies it. While in Chicago, for example, she insists on the reality of the 'invisible dog'—itself a reflection of her self-deception—and persuades Harry and McCord to accompany her on her visit to the sanctuary of her idol, where she dramatically lays the offering of the two chops at the feet of the cast-iron figure of the dog at the mansion in the well-heeled suburb. She apparently conceives of this ritual as a satire on bourgeois respectability, but the religious fervor with which she enacts it indicates a desire for a similar respectability and security in her own life. The cavalier way in which she disposes of the chops lies especially open to criticism when one considers the frequency with which she and Harry confront the possibility of starvation. The cast-iron Saint Bernard, lifeless yet life-imitating, to which she offers the sacrifice reflects the sterility and delusion of her obsession and contrasts with the 'lithograph of the Saint Bernard dog saving the child from the snow' (211) which hangs upon the wall of the brothel where Harry tries to purchase the 'abortion pills'.

Charlotte tries to make her life with Harry an *objet d'art*,[13] but her eventual failure resides in her implementation of that same distorted vision which informs the statues and puppets—'effigies elegant, bizarre, fantastic and perverse' (89)—which she produces for commercial purposes. In accordance with her life-denying artistic perspective, she describes the statues to Harry in terms which suggest a foetus which will never be born: 'Like something created to live only in the pitch airless dark . . . not in the rich normal nourishing air breathed off of guts full of vegetables from Oak Park and Evanston' (89). The puppets reveal even more directly than the statues the defects in Charlotte's outlook: grotesque versions of literary figures such as Quixote, Falstaff, Roxane and Cyrano, they represent the perverse manner in which these characters would have been molded had their creators' artistic visions been as askew as is Charlotte's. That these figures are 'puppets' seems negative in itself, and the implicit condemnation of Charlotte's aesthetic becomes even more evident if one compares her hate-filled versions—a Falstaff 'with the worn face of a syphilitic barber and gross with meat' or a Cyrano 'with the face of a low-comedy Jew in vaudeville, the monstrous flare of whose nostrils ceased exactly on the instant of becoming molluscs' (91)—to their altogether more genial originals.[14] Charlotte tells Harry and McCord that she wants to capture in her art 'the motion, the speed' (100) of life itself, but her static and perverse creations belie this sentiment. Her artistic outlook, like her attitude in general, remains exclusive, warped, and life-negating. Charlotte's failure in life and love accords with her own postulate that love does not die but that those unworthy of it do, the ocean of love spewing their carcasses onto the beach. All of which provides, of course, a forecast of—for the reader a flashback to—the situation in the beach cottage in the opening chapter of the book.

In that chapter Charlotte is obviously dying, and it becomes one of the functions of the remainder of the novel—including 'Old Man'—to reveal the various causes of her condition, both direct and indirect, and the circumstances attendant upon it. Her death may largely be assigned to a failure of the imagination, an inability to conceive of either happiness with a family or the richness of a love that mellows with maturity. Her flawed imagination both accounts for and stems from her misreading of those truths at the heart of literature; she tells Harry:

> 'the second time I ever saw you I learned what I had read in books but I never had actually believed: that love and suffering are the same thing and that the value of love is the sum of what you have to pay for it and any time you get it cheap you have cheated yourself.' (48)

Charlotte has ingested from her reading a rather strained romanticism and her economic index of love and suffering seems suspect at the very least, deriving from the same warped attitude as her creation of twisted figures for sale. As with the gap between her artistic theory and her sculpting, there is a marked discrepancy between her words and her actions with regard to love. Presumably she believes that the abortion and the risk of death constitute the validating 'price' of loving, but in fact the abortion emerges rather as an attempt to escape the cost in suffering involved in being a parent. Charlotte tells Harry that children 'hurt too much' (217), and the evasion of responsibility implicit in such an attitude, the desperate yearning to ward off pain by excluding others from the 'idyll' which she projects for herself and Harry, epitomizes Charlotte's selfish and immature perspective.

In a sense, then, the abortion itself constitutes merely a symptom of the malaise which plagues Charlotte throughout 'Wild

Palms'. And just as she pays lip-service to what she perceives to be the truths of literature without actually integrating them into her attitude, so does she sweep Harry into her orbit and profess the utmost regard for him without showing any genuine concern for his feelings. Charlotte may love Harry, after her fashion, but more as an agent requisite to the fulfillment of her dreams than for himself. Her misconception of Harry's emotional depth becomes evident in the promise which she extracts from her husband that he will provide Harry with the means of escaping the punishment resulting from Harry's involvement with her. That Charlotte thus attributes to Harry the properties of her own inclinations serves to reinforce the suggestion that she thinks of him only as an extension of herself: her assumption that he will wish to evade the suffering attendant upon his love demonstrates a profound misunderstanding of his disposition and potential. At the trial, when Harry is called to account for his actions, he does not even ask for mercy but simply pleads guilty.

Just as Charlotte's romanticism causes her to underestimate Harry's courage, so does the tall convict's romanticism in 'Old Man' incline him towards overestimating the virtues of his lady fair. In the comments which Faulkner made at the University of Virginia on the convict's predicament, he twice referred to the convict's having allowed himself to be 'taken over the jumps' by the frivolous woman with whom he believed himself to be in love.[15] During the convict's initial period of incarceration, he faithfully writes to his unresponsive lover until she sends a postcard showing him where she and her husband, one Vernon Waldrip, are 'honnymonning at' (339).

The convict's naiveté also appears in his using dime-store detective stories as training manuals for the aspiring criminal mastermind. He attributes the lack of success in his ludicrous version of the great train robbery not to any flaw in himself but to his having been 'lied to' by the writers of the cheap novels which he had so assiduously studied:

> the uncorporeal names attached to the stories, the paper novels . . . whom he believed had led him into his present predicament through their own ignorance and gullibility regarding the medium in which they dealt and took money for, in accepting information on which they placed the stamp of verisimilitude and authenticity . . . and retailed for money and which on actual

> application proved to be impractical and (to the convict) criminally false. (23)

The convict, as a self-designated critic, curses the writers for their imaginative and artistic deficiencies and lack of integrity, just as he later expresses outrage that the flood, a force 'with all the wealth of cosmic violence and disaster to draw from' should be 'so barren of invention and imagination, so lacking in pride of artistry and craftsmanship, as to repeat itself twice' (264). In both cases the convict-critic mistakenly projects his own imaginative bankruptcy onto the primary sources. His singular determination to apply with absolute literalness facts which he has garnered from the pulp books and to draw from his reading only those details which he considers pertinent to his own objectives betrays him as a reader and critic. It also precipitates a profound distrust of language and an ingrained fear of experience after his absurd misapplication of his reading reveals to him the absence of a strict correspondence between the minutiae of circumstance in fiction and the results to be expected from a formulaic transferal of those minutiae to real life situations.

In the story 'Motherhood' in *The Triumph of the Egg*, which Faulkner considered to be one of its author's best books, Anderson describes the womb as a prison[16]; in 'Old Man' Faulkner reverses the terms of the metaphor, Parchman prison representing the security of the womb for the tall convict. Unlike the reporter in *Pylon* who wants to escape the mundane predictability of life in New Valois, the convict in 'Old Man' remains obsessed with his intention of returning to the stability afforded by the unvarying regimen of prison. The extremism with which each pursues his goal, however, renders both characters equally open to censure. The convict's ardent desire to return to the womb-sanctuary of the penitentiary, his obtuse insistence on doing things 'by the book'—literally and figuratively—and his remarkable lack of imagination seem at first to render him an unlikely candidate as an artist-figure.

Such a configuration nevertheless emerges as one of the prominent features in the general relationship between 'Wild Palms' and 'Old Man'. The description of the immense power of the flood which sweeps away the tall convict bears a noteworthy resemblance to many of Faulkner's comments on the creative impulse: he often remarked on the writer's being 'demon-driven' and 'elected' to write,[17] implying that the force of the impulse itself lies to a large extent beyond the writer's control—though that would be less true of what he produces after the first wave of inspiration has receded. The convict is both 'demon-driven' by the flood and 'elected' by circumstance to accept responsibility for the woman and, eventually, her offspring: once the pregnant woman more or less drops into his lap, he finds himself forced to assume what is, in essence, the burden of creativity. In this regard, Faulkner's consistent association of motion with life and literature adds an extra dimension to the convict's estimation of the pregnant woman as a 'millstone which the force and power of blind and risible Motion had fastened upon him' (335). Although the tall convict accepts this burden for the moment, he tries desperately to rid himself of it or deny its existence—all to no avail. In many respects, the convict's predicament corresponds to a writer's nightmare: seized by a force over which he has little control, chosen to be the recipient of an assignment he neither sought nor enjoys, he nevertheless remains obligated to perform his task as competently as possible in order to preserve both his good name (that, ironically, is one of the anonymous convict's chief concerns) and his self-esteem.

The convict's attitude toward the woman as unnecessary baggage, an impediment to his ultimate goal that must nevertheless be honorably disposed of, may reflect Faulkner's feelings about the work he had so recently been doing in Hollywood: it is perhaps significant in this regard that, prior to their actual meeting, the convict imagines the woman to be a 'living Garbo' (149). Yet although there are a number of other hints of ironic self-portraiture, Faulkner's narrative technique effectively distances him from any close association with the implicit artistic attitudes and practices of his character. While the convict's very act of narration serves to consolidate his characterization as an artist-figure, the sharp distinction between his laconic relation of the story to his cell-mates and the flamboyant prose of 'Old Man' ensures that the reader gets not the convict's but Faulkner's version of the story.[18] The resulting contrast emphasises that the former's mistrust of verbal expression precludes the possibility of his recounting the experience with richness and vitality. For example, he initially compresses the entire episode with the Cajun into a single sentence: 'After a while we come to a house and we stayed there eight or nine days then they blew up the levee with dynamite so we had to leave' (252). Although later prompted by the plump convict to elaborate upon the episode, the tall convict still neglects to mention the most crucial aspects of the encounter. His doggedly literal version of the episode (and of his journey as a whole) demonstrates that although he relates the sequence of events he remains unable to grasp the meaning—a meaning which, Faulkner implies, can be comprehended and transmitted only by verbal exploration and extrapolation. The tall convict's deficiencies as an artist-figure reflect his general failure to come to terms with life: so far as possible he shuns new experience in favor of a retreat to the prison and the security of its rigid regimentation.

Since the Mississippi, with its enormous potential for both destruction and revitalization, serves as so apt a symbol for the surge of artistic inspiration, the convict's incessant battling against the current in a frantic effort to return to prison may be seen to correspond to his obstinate resistance to the creative impulse. Despite his aversion to the entire process, however, circumstances force him to participate in one of the central generative acts in the novel, the birth of the country woman's child.

The fact that this child is born on an island in the midst of the raging torrent implies in part that artistic achievement must combine the intensity that Charlotte advocates with the order that the convict craves. Faulkner once stated that inspiration and discipline were the two components essential to the creative process, and in the same interview asserted that 'A great book is always accompanied by a painful birth'.[19] Thus, Faulkner's presentation of the island as a sort of Peaceable Kingdom serves as an analogy for the fructive harmony necessary to—and engendered by—artistic conception and production.

The metal lid used by the convict in assisting at the birth reinforces his presentation as an artist-figure, especially in light of Faulkner's repeated remarks in interviews on the writer's employing any 'tool' at hand to facilitate the creative process; that the convict employs a crude implement to assist at an actual birth accords with his absurdly literal perspective. He also utilizes a variety of objects as replacements for the paddle, and his patient care in fashioning them resembles an artist's trying to perfect and polish his work and supplies as well a distinct contrast to Charlotte's whirlwind sculpting in 'Wild Palms'. The convict is so painstaking, however, that he never completes the shaping of any of the substitute paddles. On one level, this may reflect Faulkner's belief that true works of art are never finished, that they all fail, and that the artist should be judged on the basis of aspiration rather than production; on another level, however, the convict's inability to finish a paddle underscores the inadequacy of his outlook. He works most determinedly during those brief respites from the flood's intensity while on the island and, later, in Cajun country. And there are hints that his experiences during the nine days that he hunts with the Cajun bear an ironic correspondence to Faulkner's own literary apprenticeship period in New Orleans, particularly with regard to his relationship with Sherwood Anderson.[20]

In an essay published in 1953 Faulkner related that while in New Orleans in the twenties he observed Sherwood Anderson's daily schedule of working in the morning, talking in the afternoon, and drinking and talking in the evening, and thereupon decided: 'If this is what it takes to be a novelist, then that's the life for me'.[21] This response resembles the effect produced when the convict sees the hide nailed to the Cajun's wall: *'So that's it. That's what he does in order to eat and live'* (255).[22] The convict serves an apprenticeship under the Cajun much as Faulkner learned from Anderson, and the convict's and Cajun's agreement to go 'halves' on the alligator skins is suspiciously reminiscent of those Jackson stories—also dealing with alligators in the swampland—on which Faulkner and Anderson collaborated and which at one time they may have intended to publish jointly.[23] The convict's attitude towards the Cajun also seems to approximate, on whatever reductive level, that which Faulkner presumably maintained towards Anderson; the convict remarks to himself: *'If that's it, then I can do it too and even if he cant tell me how I reckon I can watch him and find out'* (257). The further comment, *'What? What? I not only dont know what I am looking for, I dont even know where to look for it'* (257) and the Cajun's subsequently showing the convict where to hunt may even allude to Faulkner's attributing to Anderson much of the impetus for his discovery of his 'own little postage stamp of native soil'.[24]

The convict also thinks: *'Only if he could just tell me what to do it would save time'* (258). Quite literally, though, because of the language barrier between them the Cajun cannot tell the convict what to do, just as Anderson could not dictate to Faulkner what sort of writer the latter should become: the Cajun can point the direction or teach by example, but ultimately the convict must make his own way. The differing techniques of the convict and the Cajun force them to pursue divergent channels which, significantly enough, are three times described as inky (251, 255, 257), as is the Cajun's mouth (265). Similarly intrinsic to the Anderson-Faulkner analogue is the message that the Cajun somehow communicates to the convict: 'You do not need me and the rifle; we will hinder you, be in your way' (261).

All these references seem to reflect Faulkner's admiration and appreciation of Anderson's work and advice while at the same time indicating his decision to pursue an independent course in his own fiction, as is also implicit in the Cajun's use of a rifle to garner the hides while the convict employs a knife and a club. The descriptions of the latter's tussles with the alligators relate in some ways to the artist's struggle to subdue recalcitrant material:

> he accepted the gambit which he had not elected, entered the lashing radius of the armed tail and beat at the thrashing and hissing head with his lightwood club, or this failing, embraced without hesitation the armored body itself with the frail web of flesh and bone in which he walked and lived and sought the raging life with an eight-inch knife-blade. (266)

And again:

> *After all a man cant only do what he has to do, with what he has to do it with, with what he has learned, to the best of his judgment* . . . . and [the convict] paused just for one instant while the words *It does look big* stood for just a second, unemphatic and trivial, somewhere where some fragment of his attention could see them and vanished, and stooped straddling, the knife driving even as he grasped the near foreleg, this all in the same instant when the lashing tail struck him a terrific blow upon the back. But the knife was home, he knew that even on his back in the mud, the weight of the thrashing beast longwise upon him, its ridged back clutched to his stomach, his arm about its throat, the hissing head clamped against his jaw, the furious tail lashing and flailing, the knife in his other hand probing for the life and finding it, the hot fierce gush. (258–9)

During his stay in the swamp the convict becomes much more of an active agent than the merely reactive pawn he seems to be earlier in the story. While he does not retain what he learns at the Cajun's camp, eventually returning to Parchman with no greater understanding of himself or of the world than when he left, that eight-inch knife-blade nonetheless functions for a time as if it were an implement suitable to the creation of art, and the convict's using it in 'probing for the life' sounds close to the purpose to which Faulkner put his pen.[25] In *Mosquitoes* the character named Faulkner describes himself as a liar by profession (145), and that early tongue-in-cheek remark resonates in the descriptions of the convict's attitude in 'Old Man':

> his hill-man's sober and jealous respect not for truth but for the power, the strength, of lying—not to be niggard with lying but rather to use it with respect and even care, delicate quick and strong, like a fine and fatal blade. (276)

The association of lying, writing and the blade pertains to the ironic correspondence between Faulkner and the convict. More adventurous speculation might relate the lash across the latter's back (as well as his severe sunburn) to Faulkner's own 'demon-driven' accident in which he burned his back at the Algonquin in November of 1937,[26] and see the unconventional 'primitivism' of the convict's technique as a thrust by Faulkner at his own categorization as an inspired primitive by much of contemporary opinion.[27]

That the convict must be carried bodily from the Cajun's camp demonstrates the depth of his feeling for the only location encountered during his odyssey which has stimulated his stunted imagination; yet his insistence on dragging the skiff along with him indicates that he has learned nothing from his experience. Through the course of the convict's adventures, the skiff comes to represent for him a kind of personal Ark of the Covenant, reminding him from whence he came and symbolizing the hope of the promised land, Parchman, which awaits at the end of his journey. Unlike the Hebrews in Exodus, however, the convict seeks not to escape from bondage to freedom but from freedom to bondage. Even though his habitual reluctance to speak abates for a brief time after he has returned to prison, his eventual recourse to terse and laconic modes of expression, as epitomized by his final two-word sentence at the conclusion of 'Old Man', reflects his intransigent desire for sanctuary from the outside world.

Like Faulkner himself in his early years, the convict travels from Mississippi to New Orleans and back again to Mississippi and, indeed, his Tom Sawyeresque escape from the armory may be read as a parody of Faulkner's own breaking away from a New Orleans milieu which he found incompatible with his artistic inclinations. Nevertheless, the convict's insistence on climbing out of a window rather than exploring possible avenues of escape behind doors 'leading he did not know where' (276) once again demonstrates his fear of new experience and his paucity of imagination, especially when one recalls that in *Mosquitoes* Fairchild twice compares the artistic enterprise to investigating dark rooms: 'It's a kind of dark thing. It's kind of like somebody brings you to a dark door. Will you enter that room, or not?' (248); and again, 'A voice, a touch, a sound: life going on about you unseen in the close dark

that dark room. You want to go into all
men live in. To look into all the darkened
. The melodrama of the convict's 'escape'
arlotte in 'Wild Palms' by exhibiting his
atization, an element in his character
eferences to acting and stage machinery
harlotte adopts different roles, thereby
e anarchy she ostensibly advocates, so
his generally consistent rage for order
Juan—who is mentioned in 'Wild Palms'
ife. In *Mosquitoes* Mrs Maurier describes
and an intimation of the convict's associ-
urs in *The Wild Palms* when the convict
the water corresponding precisely to Talli-
alls out of the skiff in *Mosquitoes*: while dodging
n shore, the convict dives into the water and 'all
d save his plunging unmistakable buttocks' (173).[28]
ict's apparent disdain for women is at least partially
e is not celibate even during his term at Parchman, having
sexual relations with a 'nameless and not young negress' (335)
n the prison grounds two years prior to being swept away by the flood. Inspired by those 'impossible pulp-printed fables' (149) he devours while in Parchman, he also romantically envisions an experience when he is sent to rescue the woman very different from the one ultimately occurring:

> and who to say what Helen, what living Garbo, he had not dreamed of rescuing from what craggy pinnacle or dragoned keep when he and his companion embarked in the skiff. (149)

Upon actually encountering the woman, however, the convict is overwhelmed by the discrepancy between the fiction he has created and the reality with which it must contend and so becomes obsessed with the need to dispose of the incongruity by getting rid of the woman. Having been unable to do so, he momentarily contemplates seducing her after she has given birth to the child on the island, but rejects the notion because of the nausea he feels after having witnessed her recent demonstration of fertility. His ambivalence in this regard contributes to the evidence of his inability to reconcile imagination and reality. The convict's brief affair with the married woman relates his evasion of the responsibilities for his sexual adventurism and his sterility of perspective in 'Old Man' to those similar features of Charlotte's attitude in 'Wild Palms'.

The convict's self-perpetuated cycle of frustration—especially regarding his involvement with women—falls into a pattern of sorts, and it is indicative of his self-delusion that he who is so obsessed with order should fail to detect this design in his own behaviour. His avowed contempt for women clearly marks an aspect of his self-deception, and his closing statement, 'Women, ——!', constitutes an unwitting condemnation of his willed blindness, not an instance of Faulkner's own alleged misogyny. In the typescript of *The Wild Palms* the convict's final word is followed not by an exclamation point but by a comma, which perhaps may have added an appropriate note of ambiguity to his apparently adamantine declaration.[29] The convict's self-delusion, when combined with his refusal to cultivate new experience and re-present it through language, means that in effect he has a return ticket to Parchman before he ever moves off its grounds; Faulkner himself, on the other hand, left Mississippi for New Orleans and eventually returned not only to Oxford in Lafayette County but also to Jefferson in Yoknapatawpha. With the possible exception of the brief interlude in the Louisiana swamp, the convict remains shackled by his self-imposed imaginative limitations throughout 'Old Man': like Charlotte, he not only blinds himself to the inconsistencies between his behavior and his avowed beliefs, but also fails in terms of what he considers to be the informing principle of his existence. Just as Charlotte cannot imagine a means of perpetuating the intensity of her relationship with Harry if she carries the pregnancy to term, so the convict rejects the possibility of any kind of constructive order outside the confines of the prison.

As has been noted by many commentators on *The Wild Palms*, Harry Wilbourne during his internship at the hospital very much resembles the convict in 'Old Man', especially in shunning the world of experience in favor of a womb-like security. He uses his lack of money to rationalize his timidity and make his fear palatable to himself, but this flimsy justification simply reveals that his imagination is even more impoverished than his pocketbook, as is equally evident in those transparent excuses he advances in an attempt to elude Flint's invitation to the party.

Like the convict, Harry is imprisoned by self-deception, a condition aggravated rather than alleviated by his association with Charlotte both prior to the abortion and for a time thereafter, as signified by his assertion to the doctor in Mississippi that he is a painter. Indeed, the entire relationship is founded on false premises: Charlotte deceives herself, while Harry, his sexual relationship with her being his first and last, has the 'ill-luck' not to discover 'that love no more exists just at one spot and in one moment and in one body out of all the earth and all time and all the teeming breathed, than sunlight does' (43)—unless, of course, he makes this discovery after his imprisonment. His general inexperience and isolation, typified by his virginity, figure prominently in his temporary acceptance of Charlotte's inordinately narrow perspective on love; nevertheless, the several false epiphanies he undergoes before his ultimate enlightenment in the jail indicate his potential for growth and result from his search for a combination of pattern and meaning which is finally successful.

In the first chapter of *The Wild Palms* Charlotte is dying, Harry is helpless, and the reader must adopt much the same position as does the doctor when he approaches the cottage, sharing with him a sense of bafflement, curiosity, and even, perhaps, outrage—a correspondence which Faulkner emphasised by relating the entire first chapter from the doctor's point of view.[30] The curtain, or veil, of the novel rises very much in the tragic mode: the ambience is suffused with that profound and ominous sense of mystery apparent in, for example, the opening scenes of *Hamlet* and *Macbeth* and, as in both of those plays, the action is introduced from the viewpoint of peripheral characters who function primarily as a chorus, implicitly or explicitly commenting on the actions and attitudes of the main characters. The doctor and his wife form an unreliable chorus, however, as the last chapter of 'Wild Palms' demonstrates: like Ike McCaslin in the 'Delta Autumn' chapter of

Go Down, Moses, the doctor has 'forgotten so much that [he does not] remember anything [he] ever knew or felt or even heard about love'.[31] The doctor's inadequacies as commentator upon—and reader of—the situation are underscored by the emphasis in Harry's final epiphany upon the importance of remembering passion. The relationship of the doctor and his wife nonetheless serves as a foil against which both the grandeur and the waste of Charlotte and Harry's liaison emerges.

Kierkegaard maintains that 'if the age loses the tragic it gains despair',[32] and the catharsis effected in Harry by Charlotte's death illustrates the manner by which a recognition of tragic implications can surmount despair. Central to our understanding *The Wild Palms* is the specific meaning which the term 'tragedy' had for Faulkner himself; as he noted at the University of Virginia: 'I don't think Aristotle meant by high place what it sounds like. I think he meant a man of integrity, more than a man of aristocracy.'[33] While certainly no aristocrat, Harry does abandon his integrity as a physician when he agrees to perform abortions on Billie Buckner and Charlotte, and his self-development, particularly with regard to the latter operation, hinges upon his recognition of the professional and moral implications of his actions. Thus Faulkner's personal views on abortion, whatever they may have been, do not pertain to the issue at hand, the point being that Harry perceives of the abortions as a casting away of the last vestiges of his personal and professional honor. By violating his ethics in an attempt to lead the life Charlotte insists that he lead, by doing hack-work as a doctor, by agreeing to perform the abortions, Harry discards an essential part of himself and takes the life of the only person whom he has ever loved. With regard to the abandoned title of *The Wild Palms*—'If I Forget Thee Jerusalem'—the 'Jerusalem' Harry has forgotten is, at one level, his self-respect and principles, and when his right hand thereby loses its cunning the results are indeed tragic for all concerned.

The Psalm from which this abandoned title was paraphrased can apply directly to a sense of artistic integrity, and there seems little doubt that Faulkner interpreted it as such:[34]

> How shall we sing the LORD's song in a
> strange land?

> If I forget thee, O Jersualem, let my right hand forget *her cunning*.
>
> If I do not remember thee, let my tongue cleave to the roof of my mouth; if I prefer not Jerusalem above my chief joy.

In a letter to Robert Haas concerning editorial bowdlerization of *The Wild Palms* Faulkner defended his original version on the basis of his desire to maintain his sense of values as an artist:

> But these words are exactly the ones which my characters would have used and no other, and there are a few people whom I hope will read the book, among whom the preservation of my integrity as a faithful (even though not always successful) portrayer of living men and women is dear enough to me to wish not to betray it, even in trifles.[35]

This high personal standard can be contrasted with Harry's dismissal of all such standards, not only as a doctor but as an artist, for Harry is indeed an artist-figure. Both Harry and the convict function throughout most of their respective sections as Jamesian centers of consciousness; and just as Buckworth's statement in the last chapter that the convict is 'up yonder in that bunkhouse right now, lying his head off probly' (326) relates to the convict's position as nominal narrator of much of 'Old Man', so one can read 'Wild Palms'—including the first chapter—as Harry's retelling of the story of Charlotte and himself and, consequently, as a product of the positive value of memory which constitutes his redemption after Charlotte's death.[36] The double-meaning of the word 'bust' in Harry's remark '*I have made a bust even of that part of my life which I threw away*' (283)—a pun, significantly enough, also operative in *Mosquitoes* with relation to Gordon—subtly anticipates Harry's emergence as an artist-figure at the conclusion of 'Wild Palms' as he comes to use his experiences with Charlotte in the creation of what is, in essence, a literary artifact. Unlike the tall convict in the final chapter of 'Old Man', Harry by the end of 'Wild Palms' has become capable of imbuing his story with life, of refusing to shift the blame for the tragedy onto anyone else, and of recognizing the complexities accompanying human experience.

Initially, however, Harry seems far from being an exemplary artist-figure: certainly his composition of those 'sexual gumdrop[s]'

(123) in Chicago should be interpreted as negative, and the literary pabulum which he produces relates to Charlotte's figurines in terms of perversity of characterization, capitulation to commercialism, infidelity to human experience, and renunciation of artistic integrity. Even though he comes to enjoy the writing of these 'primer-bald moronic fable[s]' (123)—which resemble, presumably, those to which the convict is addicted—he eventually forsakes them, an act constituting a step in his growth towards that rebirth which occurs in the jail cell in New Orleans. The convict's return to prison signifies a retreat into the womb; Harry's acceptance of his grief after being jailed provides a birth of resolution and courage. When Harry leaves Chicago, he takes along the typewriter he had used to compose his 'moron's pap' (122), and one can perhaps imagine him using that same typewriter to a much better purpose in composing 'Wild Palms' while in prison. Writing, as Faulkner claimed in various interviews, furnishes the best means of saying 'no' to death, which is precisely what Harry wants to do in affirmation of his relationship with Charlotte.

Before Harry attains enlightenment in prison, his preceding epiphanies, most notably those occurring in Wisconsin and Chicago, prove illusory in light of subsequent events—a pattern, incidentally, remarkably similar to that experienced by Stephen Dedalus in Joyce's *Kunstlerroman, A Portrait of the Artist as a Young Man*. As he leaves Chicago, Harry tells McCord:

> 'And something I told myself up there at the lake . . . . That there is something in me she is not mistress to but mother. Well, I have gone a step farther. . . . That there is something in me you and she parented between you, that you are father of. Give me your blessing.' (141)

Although the imagery in this passage does anticipate Harry's eventual rebirth in the concluding chapter of 'Wild Palms', his groping here towards the solution to his dilemma remains unsuccessful, as McCord recognizes and signifies by responding 'Take my curse.' Harry has remained heavily dependent on Charlotte, and their mutual dependence on McCord is suggested in the umbilical resonances of his name.

At this point in Harry's development, he continues to be incapable of living independently of Charlotte, or even of effectively asserting his will against hers; nevertheless, with the tragic exception of the decision to perform the abortions, Harry grows progressively stronger as an individual and more distinct as a character separate from Charlotte as 'Wild Palms' proceeds. In accordance with this progression, the focus of the novel as a whole gradually shifts from an implicit comparison between Charlotte and the convict to one between Harry and the convict—a shift which culminates in Harry's and the convict's both being imprisoned, but enduring their sentences with very different attitudes. While the convict's return to prison signifies a truncation of any imaginative potential he may have possessed, Harry's ultimate acceptance of his grief in the jail cell allows him to achieve a mature and authentic perspective on his past and present.

Harry's fumbling attempts to extract significance from his personal experience in the earlier part of 'Wild Palms' anticipates his periods of 'false labor' occurring shortly after he has been imprisoned: he twice comes near to formulating the solution but cannot quite do so. The major distinction resides in the fact that in the later attempts Harry does not try to force the meaning or the pattern to emerge as he had done in the earlier:

> that was the first time when he almost touched it. But not yet: and that was all right too; it would return; he would find it, hold it, when the time was ready. (312)

And again:

> That was the second time he almost got it. But it escaped him again. But he was not trying yet; it was still all right, he was not worried; it would return when the time was ready and even stand still to his hand. (316)

Thus, in regard to Harry's position as an artist-figure, his problem in the earlier portions of 'Wild Palms' contrasts directly with that of the convict in 'Old Man': whereas the convict is besieged by a superabundance of inspiration and mistakenly struggles against it, Harry finds himself afflicted with a paucity of inspiration and mistakenly strives for it. Likewise, once the convict has his material defined, he must (literally) wrestle with it; Harry, on the other hand, must remain patient until the moment arrives for the 'simple falling of a jumbled pattern' (323).

Memory provides one of the keys to the coherent organization of this 'jumbled pattern', but alone it remains insufficient unless it be provided with a vehicle, a container, which, according to Harry's precept is 'the old frail eradicable meat' (316). In his first instance of remembering early in 'Wild Palms', Harry meditates upon his past 'with that peace with which a middleaged eunuch might look back upon the dead time before his alteration, at the fading and (at last) edgeless shapes which now inhabited only the memory and not the flesh' (34). This dissociation emasculates and anaesthetizes Harry's memory, making the figures inhabiting it 'edgeless'; the reassociation of memory and flesh in his determination to remember Charlotte ensures that the memory, and the grief, will remain sharp and poignant—a combination and result equally significant for the writer. Indeed, the relationship between memory and flesh as determined by Harry bears an analogical correspondence to more specifically authorial concerns, such as the relationship between style and structure, or that between word and origin. Harry's epiphany occurs only after he has structured the meaning of his and Charlotte's relationship verbally. The incapacity of language to recapture presence accounts for one of the primary aspects of the 'grief' which Harry accepts. In this respect his celebrated declaration *'Yes . . . between grief and nothing I will take grief'* (324) indicates that while words form an irredeemably inadequate substitute for presence, a condition of difference which by its very nature entails the grief of loss, the determination to endure even in light of this recognition, to continue using language because the alternative is oblivion, constitutes the affirmation of the creative artist.

Another famous literary figure—created by an author with whose works Faulkner was quite familiar—who chooses grief rather than nothing is Raskolnikov in Dostoevsky's *Crime and Punishment*, and his redemption resembles Harry's in *The Wild Palms* in several respects. Certainly, Harry's feeling of suffocation in the interim between Charlotte's death from the botched abortion and his pleading guilty at the trial shares a pronounced affinity with Raskolnikov's intense claustrophobia after he stabs to death Alyona, the pawnbroker—a claustrophobia alleviated, like Harry's, only by his confession. More importantly, perhaps, Raskolnikov's situation in the much misunderstood 'Epilogue' to *Crime and Punishment* anticipates that of Harry at the end of 'Wild Palms'; in Dostoevsky's novel, the boundless vistas of the Siberian labor camp to which Raskolnikov is transported after his confession come to represent the expanded perspective ultimately resulting from his acceptance of the responsibility for the murder and the pain concomitant with that acceptance; similarly, implicit in the conclusion to 'Wild Palms' is Harry's removal to the prison farm of Parchman where, unlike the convict, he will—figuratively speaking—plow no sterile furrow but will instead sow the fertile seeds of memory and imagination.

The esteem in which Faulkner held the story of Harry's essentially artistic affirmation may be seen in the fact that he at one time suggested that 'Wild Palms' be placed in a single text alongside his personal favorite among the Yoknapatawpha novels, *The Sound and the Fury*. Robert Linscott of Random House had proposed to Faulkner that *The Sound and the Fury* and *As I Lay Dying* be combined into one volume. However, in March of 1946—at a time when, because of his recent involvement in helping Malcolm Cowley put together materials for *The Portable Faulkner*, Faulkner presumably had the intertextuality of his canon up to that point in mind—he responded:

> I dont agree with you about printing TSAF and AS I LAY DYING together. . . . I would like to see TSAF and THE WILD PALMS section from that book, the part of it about the doctor who performed the abortion on his own sweetheart.[37]

Faulkner's suggestion was never followed and, in fact, *The Sound and the Fury* and *As I Lay Dying* were eventually published together as Modern Library No. 187. But to speculate on the effect which would have been produced by such a linkage of 'Wild Palms' and *The Sound and the Fury* is to arrive at a clearer and fuller appreciation both of Faulkner's perception of his canon and of his aesthetic as a whole. The proposed volume, for instance, would have served to underscore Faulkner's insistence that even apparently disparate and discrete texts in his canon are related one to another and so constitute segments of a unified corpus.[38] Despite the fact that *The Sound and the Fury* is set primarily in Yoknapatawpha while 'Wild Palms' makes no direct reference to Faulkner's fictional county, the two texts have striking and fundamental correspondences. Indeed, it seems entirely possible that Faulkner was subtly and deliberately invoking the story of the Compsons while composing *The Wild Palms* in order to provide both works with an intertextual version of that quality of counterpoint which figures so prominently in each when considered in isolation.

Quentin's is in many ways the central section of *The Sound and the Fury*, and it also seems the portion of that novel which relates most specifically to 'Wild Palms'. Quentin may even be seen as a touchstone by which the attributes and defects of the major characters in 'Wild Palms' can be viewed in perspective: the affinities which Quentin shares with Charlotte Rittenmeyer and with the middle-aged doctor in Mississippi suggest the extent to which the attitudes of all three are life-denying. By contrast, Harry Wilbourne's progression in 'Wild Palms' from a position very much resembling Quentin's in *The Sound and the Fury* to one diametrically opposite in its affirmation of grief, memory and life serves to delineate those crucial differences in perspective which distance Harry from Quentin, Charlotte, the doctor, and, indeed, the tall convict in 'Old Man'.

In the early sections of 'Wild Palms' Harry resembles not only the doctor in that same story but also Quentin in *The Sound and the Fury*: he is weak, emotionally insecure, and frightened of experience. There are also numerous specific correspondences between Harry and Quentin which suggest that Faulkner was in a sense encouraging the reader familiar with both works to compare and contrast the two characters. For example, the two bricks which Harry carries to his and Charlotte's first assignation call to mind the two flat-irons which Quentin uses as weights when he drowns himself in the Charles River, and there may even be an oblique relation between the name of that river and the name of the lover in whose will Harry becomes so deeply immersed: Charlotte is on at least one occasion referred to as 'Charley' (38), and is consistently associated throughout 'Wild Palms' with water imagery and even with the idea of death by water (58).[39] When Harry and Charlotte meet for the first time, he is described as 'drowning, volition and will' in her 'yellow stare' (39).[40] In the 'Compson Appendix', written after *The Wild Palms* had been published, Faulkner employs similar terms in describing Quentin as 'relinquishing, drowning' in his love of death.[41]

In fact, many of Quentin's remarks in *The Sound and the Fury* resonate with the tone, rhythm and imagery of Harry's subsequent encomium to the peace of drowning:

'This is a solitude. Then the water wavering slow while you lie

> and look up at it. . . . And then you could open your eyes for a minute if you wanted to, remembered to, and watch the shadow of the rocking leaves on the breast beside you.' (*The Wild Palms*, 100)

Harry even constructs what amounts to his own paraphrase of Quentin's '*Non fui. Sum. Fui. Non sum.*'[42] pronouncement: '*I was not*. Then *I am*, and time begins, retroactive, is was and will be. Then *I was* and so I am not and so time never existed' (137, Faulkner's italics). And just as Quentin contemplates castration as a possible solution to his dilemma, so does Harry review his life with the 'peace [of] a middleaged eunuch' (34). Indeed, the description of Harry's mental state while serving as an intern in New Orleans, his recalling of his previous years 'as though he floated effortless and without volition upon an unreturning stream' and his peopling the memories of those years with 'the fading and (at last) edgeless shapes which now inhabited only the memory and not the flesh' (34), might aptly characterize Quentin's attitude throughout the second section of *The Sound and the Fury*.

Ultimately, however, Harry's arriving at the epiphanic insight that he must bind together memory and flesh to ensure vitality in the present contrasts directly with Quentin's committing suicide partly in order to dissolve that very bond. And although Harry initially resembles Quentin in being an effete and ineffectual virgin, his consenting—however passively—to involvement in a relationship with Charlotte underscores an openness to experience that Quentin lacks. As Faulkner remarks in the 'Compson Appendix', Quentin's infatuation with death renders him 'incapable of love',[43] and this is a primary factor in his suicide; Harry, on the other hand, tells McCord that he would never commit suicide because he 'still believe[s] in love' (101).

Indeed, despite the many correspondences between Harry and Quentin, the intertextual relationship between the two ultimately emerges as one of opposition. Given this fact—along with the importance of birth imagery in *The Wild Palms* as a whole—it seems particularly significant that Harry should be born in 1910, the same year in which Quentin commits suicide. In many ways, Quentin's tragic terminus, particularly with regard to his attitude towards life itself, constitutes Harry's starting point, each of the several false epiphanies which the latter experiences carrying him another stage beyond Quentin's death-ridden outlook and marking a step forward on his journey towards understanding, towards an acceptance of that complexity inherent in life which Quentin so furiously and futilely tries to deny.

The ironic inversions related to the circumstances surrounding the stories of Quentin and Harry highlight the distinctions between them. For example, at one point Quentin intends to kill Caddy and then himself with a knife, yet finds himself unable to act at the crucial moment. Harry, on the other hand, has no intention of killing Charlotte, yet he inadvertently does so with the knife used to perform the abortion. Caddy's becoming pregnant is the indirect cause of Quentin's death, whereas the fatally botched abortion in 'Wild Palms' becomes the catalyst for Harry's spiritual rebirth in Parchman. Quentin commits suicide while Harry endures, even though the latter's predicament is in many ways the more desperate: Caddy at least remains alive, while Harry must come to terms not only with Charlotte's death but with his own complicity in it. Both Quentin and Harry are put on trial: the former is innocent yet becomes convulsed with hysterical laughter; the latter is guilty of a much more serious offense, yet his admission of guilt is notable for its stoic acceptance of responsibility. Quentin is released through the intervention of friends only to drown himself later that same day; Harry, despite Rat Rittenmeyer's appeal for clemency, receives a sentence of fifty years' hard labor which plays a part in his spiritual rejuvenation when back in his cell shortly after the trial. Quentin, not unlike the tall convict in 'Old Man', remains primarily a prisoner of his own neurotic obsessions. Harry, by contrast, faces a seemingly interminable stretch of physical confinement in prison but nevertheless rejects that very alternative of suicide for which Quentin opts, ultimately freeing his imagination sufficiently to arrive at that most unequivocally affirmative epiphany in the entire Faulkner canon: '*Yes,* he thought, *between grief and nothing I will take grief*' (324, Faulkner's italics).[44]

Even Harry's surname may be seen as emphasizing the distinction between Quentin and himself. 'Wilbourne' calls to mind Hamlet's reference to 'The undiscovered country, from whose bourn/No traveller returns, [which] puzzles the will', the first syllable of Harry's surname perhaps also relating to Shakespeare's—and presumably in this instance Faulkner's—tendency to pun on his own first name. The Hamlet allusion, of course, may be traced to the 'To be or not to be' soliloquy, and the decision Hamlet confronts as to whether or not he should commit suicide is precisely that faced by both Harry and Quentin, the former ultimately choosing 'to be', the latter—whose interior monologue bears many allusions to Shakespeare's play—deciding irrevocably 'not to be'. As a consequence of Quentin's determination to take his own life, his interior monologue captures the dissolution of his own sense of individuality, as is suggested by the use of the lower-case 'i' for the personal pronoun towards the conclusion of his section in *The Sound and the Fury*. Harry's story in 'Wild Palms', on the other hand, involves the gradual emergence of a firm conception of his identity, which ultimately enables him to accept both the responsibility for Charlotte's death and the moral imperative to preserve whatever remnant of life she may in memory possess.

Quentin's use of memory, unlike Harry's, is death-oriented, and although his monologue in *The Sound and the Fury* elicits some sympathy, it also betrays a rather maudlin sentimentality. While Mrs Compson's refusal to provide Quentin with maternal affection is indeed tragic, his repeatedly lamenting this deprivation reflects his self-pity and the ineffectual romanticism from which it stems. There is some indication that Harry has also been denied the security of a mother's love—his mother is never mentioned in 'Wild Palms'—yet he overcomes the potentially devastating aspects of his predicament by distancing himself from it. The opening sentence of one of those 'sexual gumdrops' written in Chicago relates to his and Quentin's mutual predicament: Harry's 'If I had only had a mother's love to guard me on that fatal day' (121) forms an ironic counterpart to Quentin's *'if I'd just had a mother so I could say Mother Mother'*.[45] Indeed, the differing contexts in which these two similar statements are couched provide an insight into the self-pity underlying what might otherwise in Quentin's soliloquy seem so emotionally evocative a refrain. Both Quentin and Harry confront that dilemma which Faulkner in *Go Down, Moses* refers to as 'the tragic complexity of . . . motherless childhood',[46] and their differing responses to it typify their varying attitudes to the 'tragic complexity' of life itself: Quentin capitulates to this complexity through his refusal to develop the inner resources necessary to come to terms with it, thus choosing nothing over grief; Harry eventually triumphs through his acceptance of the intricacy of the human condition—an acceptance which involves the recognition that if grief and nothing are the only alternatives, the former is preferable by far to the latter.

Harry's ultimate confirmation of the value of life, however tragic, and his related configuration as a successful artist-figure depend heavily upon his using language to confront, to discover, meaning. As 'Wild Palms' proceeds Harry's remarks become increasingly coherent and to the point, his strained and disjointed metaphysical speculations when with McCord eventually yielding to the insight later achieved not through 'a flash of comprehension' (323) but rather by his allowing for that 'simple falling of a jumbled pattern' (323)—a resolution which occurs, significantly enough, in conjunction with his refusal to take the cyanide proffered by Rat Rittenmeyer. The movement of Quentin's interior monologue in *The Sound and the Fury*, on the other hand, may be described—in André Bleikasten's apt term—as entropic,[47] becoming increasingly fragmented and impenetrable despite the illusion of order and coherence invoked at its conclusion. Whereas Harry finally succeeds in deciphering and, indeed, in conveying truth because he allows meaning to emerge from experience, Quentin fails as a narrator—as, in effect, an author—because of his vain attempt to channel experience into a preconceived system which, precisely because it remains so inflexible, partakes (in Faulknerian terms) of the stasis of death rather than of the motion of life.

Indeed, Quentin's narrative failings and his obsessive desire to seek security by shunning experience much more closely resemble the tall convict's tendencies than Harry's. At a point late in his interior monologue, Quentin recalls that in reference to a picture in a children's book he and Caddy had read he had felt that 'the dungeon was Mother herself'.[48] Quentin seems to associate this dungeon with the peace which he now desires, and the monologue as a whole suggests that Quentin drowns himself in order to regain an amniotic security through his death by water. Quentin's throwing himself into the womb-tomb of the Charles River may thus be associated with the tall convict's carrying out his equally adamantine resolution to return to the womblike security of his 'dungeon', Parchman. And in their respective narratives, both the convict and Quentin fail to maintain any fidelity to the complexity of human conduct because each refuses to recognize it in his own experience.

In spite of the many obscurities in the Quentin section of *The Sound and the Fury*, it gradually becomes evident to the reader that Quentin's narrative is the product of an essentially reductive perspective. The 'characters' he presents remain one-dimensional, mere shades capable only of antic and meaningless gestures because his own disturbed state deprives them of motivation and feeling. Quentin thus is not only a poor player but a poor narrator, his obsessive concentration upon what might be termed the neurotic nodes of his discourse indicating that his outlook is dominated by them to the exclusion of all else. That Quentin relates present action in the past tense implies that in a sense he is dead to the present prior to his actual suicide,[49] his perspective having become submerged in a past which he refuses to relinquish, confront, or rise above. He thus condemns himself to existing in a shadow realm of the past which devitalizes the present and abrogates the future. Quentin's is the voice of one already dead, his interior monologue constituting in essence a lengthy suicide note which helps to explain—but certainly not to justify—his infatuation with death.

Whereas Quentin's narrative is marked by an increasing constriction of perspective, Harry's outlook in 'Wild Palms' becomes progressively more expansive, those false epiphanies to which he arrives *en route* to his climactic choice of grief over nothing providing proof of his openness to experience—and to experiment. Harry consistently uses language as a means of exploring life, of attempting to perceive significance, and hence his final epiphany depends, importantly enough, upon his ability to 'think it into words' (323). Regardless of how banal, confused, or derivative some of his remarks early in the novel may be, they are all infused with the vitality of process, of an attitude and mode of expression charged with possibilities for alteration, modification, and refinement. Unlike Quentin, Harry permits meaning to emerge through language, to be coincident with expression. If Quentin and Harry may each be considered a portrait of the artist as a young man, the intertextual contrast between the two characters highlights the reasons for the former's failure and the latter's attaining at least the potential for success.

The juxtaposition in a single volume of *The Sound and the Fury*, Faulkner's favorite Yoknapatawpha novel, and 'Wild Palms', the work which in many ways forms the epitomization of his non-Yoknapatawpha material, would have illustrated the similarities and differences between the treatments of the perennial themes of his literature within and beyond the boundaries of his fictional county; it would also have provided an apt demonstration of the intertextual relationships prevailing within his canon as a whole. The radical differences between the two works, combined with the implicit insistence on an overarching relationship between them, would have made the proposed volume quintessentially Faulknerian—as, indeed, is *The Wild Palms* itself. In 'Wild Palms', Harry Wilbourne eventually succeeds in determining the significance in the 'jumbled pattern' of his experience with Charlotte; the volume proposed in 1946 would perhaps have induced readers to try to perceive the fundamental unity in what was for so long considered to be the 'jumbled pattern' of Faulkner's own canon. Only now is substantial progress being made in that direction, and in the process *The Wild Palms* is emerging as central to an understanding of the relationships existing among all of Faulkner's works.

6

A Fable

Writing to Harold Ober in December of 1947 about the manuscript of *A Fable*, Faulkner asserted: 'There is nothing wrong with the book as it will be, only it may be 50 years before the world can stop to read it'.[1] During the long course of the composition of *A Fable* it must at times have seemed to Faulkner that it would take him almost that long just to write the novel: he worked intermittently on it for over ten years, from the fall of 1943 to the spring of 1954.[2]

As the acknowledgement which precedes the text of *A Fable* indicates, the 'basic idea' for the book originated with Henry Hathaway and William Bacher, two of Faulkner's associates in Hollywood. Faulkner was to write a movie script based on the concept of the Unknown Soldier being a latter-day Christ; Hathaway would direct the film and Bacher produce it, Faulkner retaining the right to make use of the idea in whatever fictive form he found suitable. He originally had a short story or novella in mind,[3] but gradually recognized the need for a larger framework to accommodate his idea. During its early stages, Faulkner tentatively entitled the work 'Who?' in keeping with his original plan of revealing the Christ-Corporal analogy through understatement, of providing hints concerning the correspondence in the early chapters but not developing them explicitly until the latter part of the novel. By mid-April of 1946, however, he had rejected both this strategy and the working title, and by 1948, according to Malcom Cowley, he had settled on 'A Fable' as the title of his work in progress.[4]

Almost from its inception *A Fable* proved problematic for Faulkner: seeming unsure of the tack he wished to take, he subjected the manuscript to an extraordinary number of rewritings and revisions. Keen Butterworth has suggested that Faulkner's difficulties with the book stemmed primarily from the idea's having originated with Hathaway and Bacher rather than with Faulkner himself,[5] a view indirectly supported by a remark which Faulkner made in a 1945 letter to Ober concerning a proposal that he do a book on the Mississippi River:

> I would like to do it, if I believed I could do a first rate job. I would have no qualms about the first rate job, if I had thought of the idea myself. But as I have not thought of such a book in my 47 years, perhaps the job is not for me.[6]

Whatever the reasons for his difficulties in writing the fable, there were frequent interruptions in the course of its composition; some self-imposed, as when he set aside the manuscript to work on *Intruder in the Dust* (1948), *Knight's Gambit* (1949), and *Requiem for a Nun* (1951); others, such as his trip to Sweden in 1950 to accept the Nobel Prize, the result of his growing reputation as a writer.

Perhaps because of the problems he was having with the completion of his fable, Faulkner frequently expressed an uncharacteristic insecurity about the quality of the work he was doing. The positive assessments implied in his calling the work his 'epic poem' and his 'magnum o'[7] would often be qualified by doubts regarding his ability to judge its merits accurately. This atypical equivocation appears, for example, in a letter which Faulkner wrote to Bennett Cerf and Robert Haas at Random House in 1945:

> I am doing a thing [*A Fable*] which I think is pretty good. Unless I am wrong about it, have reached that time of an artist's increasing years when he no longer can judge what he is doing, I have grown up at last.[8]

Although this letter was written at a fairly early stage in the genesis of *A Fable*, the same hesitation to make an unreserved estimation of the manuscript's quality appears in a letter of August 1953 to Saxe Commins: 'It is either nothing and I am blind in my dotage, or it is the best of my time'.[9] After the book's publication on 2 August 1954, Faulkner remarked that he considered it to be a good work in general, but 'weak in spots'.[10]

This relative disappointment may well have been a manifestation of Faulkner's customary feeling that each of his works was in some sense a 'failure'; his reaction nonetheless closely corresponds to the reception of *A Fable* at the time it was first published. Most of the early analyses concentrated on the Christ-Corporal analogue, many suggesting that the Corporal was too ill-defined to carry the weight of the Christ symbolism. Some, although admitting the power of certain passages, found themselves vexed by Faulkner's rhetoric. Several faulted the book's 'theology', while others objected to the number of sub-plots and to the dominating presence of the generalissimo. Some of the early reviews and critiques, notably Heinrich Straumann's and Sylvan Schendler's, were more sympathetic but few presented unqualified praise.[11]

More recent commentary has emphasised Faulkner's humanism rather than his 'theology' and devoted some consideration to the subtle structural framework which underlies the sequence of, and the links between, the many fables in *A Fable*. The focus has shifted from the Corporal himself to his effect on the other characters. One point which has received much attention, and rightly so, is the manner in which Faulkner suggests the essential duality of the human condition, the ongoing warfare between the capacity for good and the capacity for evil. Despite such changes in emphasis, however, the critical consensus remains much as it was in the 1950s: that *A Fable* is powerful in conception but flawed in execution.

The very title of the novel poses a dilemma for those commentators who refer it specifically to Aesop's fables. However, in Faulkner's frequent use of the term 'fable' he seemed to have had in mind not Aesop, but something more closely akin to the Latin *fabula*, denoting legend or myth. That this was the sense he sought to convey in the title *A Fable* is further indicated by his insistence on a cross's being placed on the title page, thereby making it part of the title of the work. Thus, what Faulkner presents in the novel is a version of one of those enduring myths which constitute, as he puts it in *A Fable*, 'the firmament of man's history instead of the mere rubble of his past',[12] and his recognition that the eternal manifests itself through the ephemeral largely accounts for the prevailing narrative mode in *A Fable* of 'high rhetoric', replete with both symbolism and naturalistic detail. The creation of a myth demands—or at least permits—the use of both.

When *A Fable* is read as myth, it becomes evident that Faulkner does not present the Christ analogue 'in an orgy of unbridled sentimental obeisance to the fairy tale which conquered the Western world', to borrow McCord's remark in *The Wild Palms* (130). Rather he treats it as a recurrent mythic pattern in the eternal human story. In his interview with Jean Stein, Faulkner voiced precisely such an attitude with regard to the fable of Christ:

> It cannot teach man to be good as the text book teaches him mathematics. It shows him how to discover himself, evolve for himself a moral code and standard within his capacities and aspirations, by giving him a matchless example of suffering and sacrifice and the promise of hope. Writers have always drawn, and always will, on the allegories of moral consciousness, for the reason that the allegories are matchless.[13]

From this perspective, the war itself seems less than a central concern in *A Fable*, providing the occasion for the fable but not its meaning.

Of course, if Faulkner were to remain true to the 'basic idea' suggested by his Hollywood associates, the setting for the novel had to be France during the First World War. He may also have felt particularly inclined toward this choice because, as the opening chapter of *A Fable* indicates, Faulkner apparently viewed the First World War as a climacteric between the medieval and the modern, a whirlpool in the stream of time which had caught up cavalry and tanks, bayonets and poison gas, in its spinning vortex.[14] Of course, Faulkner's choosing in 1943, when World War II was raging throughout Europe, to become involved in a text set in wartime France suggests that the subject matter may in a general sense be considered topical, a feature which serves to align *A Fable* with those previous texts set ouside of Faulkner's fictional county; as we have seen, topicality also forms a constituent part of the four other non-Yoknapatawpha novels. Moreover, given the fact that Faulkner takes pains to suggest in *A Fable* that the World War I setting simply provides a specific context for actions whose significance transcends the limitations of time and place, we may assume that Faulkner felt that this setting would in many essential respects be as 'current' as one involving World War II. As Millgate observes, the First World War became important for Faulkner as an artist 'not so much for its own sake but rather as a source of those permanent truths, those fables of eternal validity, which he saw as inhering in all human conflict'.[15]

One of the salient features of all Faulkner's war fiction concerns the degree to which the soldiers find themselves feeling—whether at home or abroad—uprooted and displaced, strangers in a strange land. As in that earlier World War I novel, *Soldiers' Pay*, the deracination of the characters receives much emphasis in *A Fable*, Faulkner again implying that alienation is more a matter of attitude than of geography. The deracinated characters in *A Fable* are wilfully so, carrying, like Satan in Milton's *Paradise Lost*, their hell with them wherever they go. In a sense, they choose alienation through an abdication from responsibility: Gragnon, the sentry, the runner and the Norman all attempt to evade in one way or another the complexity inherent in choice. On the other hand, those whom one might expect to be deracinated—the Corporal's sister Marya in Chaulnesmont, Sutterfield in France, and the groom in America—feel perfectly comfortable in unfamiliar environs.

The dual modes of reference to the groom-sentry and Sutterfield-Tooleyman point to this distinction. In America, the groom occupies the position for which he was born, taking care of horses: his baptism by Sutterfield, his dutiful fulfillment of his religious obligations thereafter while in America, and his initiation into the Masons—all indicate his sense of community while functioning in that role. Yet, because of the grief occasioned by the death of the racehorse, the groom refuses until near the end of his life to place himself again in such a vulnerable position. Not only does he reject service as an officer's groom during the war, he also gambles on men's lives, thereby consigning to chance the responsibility for life and death. His being a sentry during the war serves to suggest his defensive, almost paranoiac, attitude after his return from America, and his attack on the runner, whose message of hope threatens the sentry's self-contained isolation, illustrates his determination to buttress his strident disavowal of man's capacity to combat evil. In contrast, Sutterfield remains perfectly willing to recognize and bear the responsibility for the human good and evil: thus, for 'Tooleyman' (*'Tout le monde'*), as Sutterfield comes to be called in France, all the world is his home.

The change of name and occupation, respectively, of Sutterfield and the groom after they arrive in France constitutes but two among many examples of Faulkner's investing the names, ranks and occupations of the characters with a symbolic significance entirely in keeping with the fabular ambience of the novel as a whole. This delineation of the characters as overtly representative seems Faulkner's way of insisting that *A Fable* be read as an essentially mythic construct embodying the eternal verities to which he devoted his career. Of course, in a sense each of Faulkner's novels can be considered fabular, and it is in fact possible to read the distinctly mythic qualities of *A Fable* as exhibiting one aspect of the novel's configuration as a complex retrospective primer to Faulkner's work in its entirety, a reading wholly consonant with his exalted ambition for the book. The seemingly disparate yet, in fact, closely interrelated fables in his *'magnum opus'* mirror in many ways the relations among the fables which comprise the canon.

At the time that Faulkner was working on *A Fable,* his previous novels had been received with a remarkable lack of sympathy and understanding, and it is perfectly conceivable that in a work for which he had such high aspirations he should respond to this dearth of comprehension by incorporating into the novel a model reflecting obliquely back to his previous output and hinting at ways in which his canon might be interpreted. Faulkner's concern at this point in his career with the ability of the reader to understand the fables of literature is demonstrated by the number of characters in *A Fable* who engage in reading of some sort.[16] The attributes and the deficiencies of such characters correspond to the varying qualities of understanding which they bring to their reading, Faulkner thus implying—as he had done in the earlier non-Yoknapatawpha texts—an ineluctable link between the ability to discern the verities embodied in literature and the capacity to maintain an adequate and authentic perspective on life.

In *A Fable,* Faulkner further associates the ability to apply to life the truths gleaned from enduring literary fables with the artistic impulse and endeavor, thereby insisting on art's relevance to human capacity for sacrifice and endurance. Although no character in the novel produces art in the conventional sense of the term, many exhibit artistic inclinations or potential—an indication that these characters not only *live* the myth but through their attitudes and actions they in a sense *write* it. Faulkner's use of major characters such as Levine and the runner as discrete Jamesian centers of consciousness reinforces this configuration and derives, in part, from an emphasis on the necessity of each character to achieve self-definition within the context of the situation, while at the same time underscoring the multivalent nature of truth and circumstance, background and experience, which impedes the fulfillment of that obligation. *A Fable* teems with subdued artist-figures—Gragnon's aide, the runner, the Norman, Sutterfield, and so on—and although no single character constitutes a portrait of *the* artist, the manner in which each interprets and responds to the fable in which all are involved demonstrates the wide range of possibility for divergent interpretation and consequent action. This use of multiple narrative perspectives provides the basis for the presentation of a series of ultimately irresolvable oppositions which emerges as a fundamental principle of *A Fable*. The generalissimo and the Corporal are in many ways the two central figures in the text, and their respective attitudes are at one and the same time mutually valid and mutually irreconcilable. The tension which results inexorably from their opposition relates to, and provides the dynamic for, the antitheses arising from the juxtaposition of those supplementary fables generated by the other artist-figures.

Gragnon's aide, one of the first artist-figures whom the reader encounters, makes his appearance prior to the temporary armistice, and the manner of his presentation in some respects anticipates that of the more important artist-figures who come into prominence later in the text. The aide is rather effeminate—he had been a couturier in peacetime;[17]—and he is also a kind of 'closet' hero-author. He tells Gragnon that he has always wanted to be brave and, having rejected the possibility of playing valiant roles upon the stage because that would have been 'just acting' (45), he decides instead to become an author and in that way satisfy his desire to demonstrate his courage.

Although his timidity and his inordinately romantic conception of the writer's vocation suggest how far the aide actually is from being an exemplary artist-figure, his reasons for reading would certainly gain *his* author's approval: they are to find out all he can about 'glory . . . and honour and sacrifice, and the pity and compassion you have to have to be worthy of honour and sacrifice, and the courage it takes to pity, and the pride it takes to deserve the courage' (45). The salutary effects of the aide's reading appear when he gives his life to save two people, one of whom eventually becomes the patroness of *Les Amis Myriades et Anonymes à la France de Tout le Monde*. Gragnon hears the story of the aide's death from a runner who was there at the time. Whether it is *the* runner who later emerges as one of the key figures in the story remains impossible to determine, but the circumstances surrounding the aide's death in any case form an ironic commentary on the blast which later maims the runner: whereas the aide's sacrifice saves two lives, the runner's self-serving manipulation results in the annihilation of two battalions.

If the runner who relates the fable of the aide's death is indeed *the* runner, then both he and Gragnon should take it as an object lesson in virtue: both, however, note the experience but miss the meaning. Gragnon, to his credit, makes an attempt to divine what the aide learned about the eternal verities from *Gil Blas*, a novel which the aide had recommended to him, but Gragnon's references to 'make-believe' (45), his inability to reconcile courage and pity, and his belief that the stories in the novel 'were inventions . . . besides being in another country and long ago and therefore even if they had been real, they could never impinge, affect, the course of his life and its destruction' (48)—all demonstrate his imperviousness not only to fiction but also to the kind of truth that transcends mere fact. His primary reaction to *Gil Blas* is amazement at 'the capacity and industry and (he admitted it) the competence of the man who could remember all this and write it down' (48). Like the tall convict in *The Wild Palms*, Gragnon's being unremittingly literal renders him utterly incapable of even entertaining the notion of a distinction between fact and fiction, the latter lying outside the bounds of his hopelessly narrow conception of the world. And again like the convict, Gragnon remains obsessed with the security provided by a strict regimentation, his obstinate denial of the imagination accounting for his inability to come to terms with any occurrence without resorting to the meticulously defined directives of the military code.

The picaresque adventures of *Gil Blas* do, however, seem a rather odd authorial choice by which to indicate Gragnon's lack of receptivity. Indeed Faulkner may have chosen the book precisely for that reason, thereby implying that any fine work of literature makes fruitful reading because each explicitly or implicitly treats the same themes and endorses the same values. If Gragnon noted nothing else in the book, he might at least have perceived Gil's flexibility, for the single trait most responsible for Gragnon's doom is his obduracy—it is at one and the same time his greatest strength and his tragic weakness. *Gil Blas* may also have appealed to Faulkner because of the way in which the primary narrative is frequently interrupted by Gil's encounters with assorted characters who recount their personal histories at great length, a structural strategy analogous to those 'interruptions' in *A Fable* which supplement and expand the meaning of its central conflict by providing additional fables for comparison and contrast.[18]

One such fable revolves around the runner who, although in a manner quite different from Gragnon's, nevertheless evinces a similar inability to grasp the truths at the core of the fables of literature. Prior to the war, the runner had been in some sense an artist: 'not only a successful architect, but a good one' and in his private life an 'aesthete and even a little precious' (60). Although a brave soldier, however, his attempt to resign his commission resembles Gragnon's attempt to do the same thing in that it constitutes in effect an effort to shirk responsibility. The ostensible reason for the runner's attempted resignation is his hatred of people, yet his 'hatred' is clearly the obverse of his idealistic love. Desperate for demotion, the runner orchestrates a bawdy scene with a young prostitute in London which forces the military hierarchy to strip him of his rank; here the runner, unlike Gragnon's aide, contents himself with being merely an actor. Moreover, as Butterworth has observed, the runner's manipulation of the London prostitute, who is 'not a professional, not really a good-standing amateur yet' (62), compares most unfavorably with the Corporal's treatment of the Marseilles whore whom he takes as wife.[19]

And although the runner's indomitable idealism contrasts sharply with the sentry's cynicism, the two characters are alike in some of their most fundamental attitudes. For example, the runner's desire to resign his commission forms an analogue to the sentry's refusal to serve as a groom during the war: the former wishes to resign in order to escape what he terms 'that sort of masturbation about the human race people call hoping' (62); the sentry desires to flee from the emotions resulting from his experience with the racehorse.

Yet just as the sentry's very nature commits him to exist perpetually in an 'aura, effluvium of stalls and tack-rooms' (57), so the runner cannot 'run' from his responsibilities,[20] the marks of the officer's insignia still visible on his uniform serving as an objective correlative for his inability to forget that he once held a commission. For example, his having been an officer makes him hesitant to approach the Corporal and his disciples; however, the Corporal's willingness to accept people as people, regardless of essentially superficial distinctions such as rank, appears as one of the most pronounced aspects of his personality and so highlights the runner's distorted perception in this regard. The runner's misreading of the Corporal and hence of the fable which unfolds before him typifies the defects in his attitude which manifest themselves in one form or another throughout the novel. The colonel's suggestion that the runner can rid himself of humanity by shooting himself in the latrines (65) anticipates Levine's manner of suicide, and it becomes clear that both Levine and the runner are disastrously misled by their respective types of idealism.

The runner's deficiencies as a reader of life and literature also appear in his misuse of the lines he recalls from Marlowe's *The Jew of Malta*. He takes the lines out of context, misquotes them, and applies them to the incident with the London prostitute in order to reassure himself that he has indeed been stripped of his commission:

> lo, I have committed fornication.
> But that was in another country; and besides,
> the wench is dead. (70)[21]

In the play, the lines epitomize Barabas's essential lack of humanity, his predilection for using other people for his own purposes and then casting them aside in a manner similar to the runner's own treatment of the London prostitute and others throughout *A Fable*. For all of the runner's vaunted idealism and love for humanity, he never expresses remorse for the dire consequences of his actions; he becomes so utterly absorbed in his ideal that he fails to recognize the death and destruction for which he is responsible. The first time that he remembers the fragment from Marlowe's play, significantly enough, he substitutes it for 'the harassing ordeal of thought' (70). The runner's equation of finance and poetry (147) seems equally suspect, as does his implied interpretation of the horsethief fable which Sutterfield provides. That he only partially comprehends the meaning of this fable becomes apparent in the contrast between his response to it and that of another artist-figure who plays a minor role in the horsethief fable itself, the ex-deputy.[22]

Just prior to Sutterfield's recitation of this fable, the runner thinks: '*A protagonist. If I'm to run with the hare and be the hounds, too, I must have a protagonist*' (151). The desire for a protagonist signifies the runner's predisposition to polarize the characters in the upcoming narrative into distinct moral categories, an attitude which inclines him to ignore the central truth contained in the tale and rendered explicit by Sutterfield's disquisition on the essential duality of human nature. The runner's mistake in expecting and demanding a readily identifiable hero may be inferred from the almost total absence of such characters in Faulkner's own texts, including *A Fable* itself. Indeed, by means of the negative example provided in the runner's narrow and self-serving response to the racehorse fable, Faulkner could well be emphasizing that classifying the characters in his fables as protagonists and antagonists leads inevitably to a misreading of his works.

The runner's choice of the deputy marshal as protagonist signifies his egocentric bias, for, as Kathryn Chittick observes, it is 'in the figure most like himself [that] he locates the parable's hero and moral exemplar.'[23] Certainly the two are similar in some respects. Both, for example, once attended Oxford; more importantly, the ex-deputy is also an artist-figure, being referred to in the text as 'a poet', although (like Gragnon's aide) 'not the writing kind, or anyway not yet, but rather still one of Homer's mere mute orphan godchildren' (158–9). Like the runner, the ex-deputy resigns when he finds his position incompatible with his ideals.

Yet the two differ markedly in their respective capacities for perception and understanding. Unlike the runner, the deputy can see the truth in the fable:

> or not even *the* truth, but *truth*, because truth was truth: it didn't have to be anything; it didn't even care whether it was so or not even, looking (the deputy) at it not even in triumph but in humility, because an old Negro minister had already seen it with one glance going on two years ago now. (159)

Rather than sifting the fable for specific facts, as the runner does, the ex-deputy views it as a whole, perceiving it (to refer once again to Faulkner's remarks to Stein) as one of those 'matchless allegories of moral consciousness' which reveal not *the* truth, as transferable to isolated personal circumstances, but *truth* as universal. The ex-deputy's refusal to predetermine the moral of the story by searching for a protagonist frees him from a constricted interpretation of the fable, and although his open response often leads him into states comprised of equal parts of bewilderment and amazement, it ultimately renders him superior to the runner as a participant in the story's re-creation. Faulkner emphasises this difference by using the deputy as an index against which the runner's imaginative involvement in the tale may be gauged: '(the runner seeing this too out of the listening, the hearing) . . . (though not as well as the Federal ex-deputy could have seen it)' (195); and again, 'the runner seeing that now almost as well as the Federal ex-deputy could have seen it' (196).

Even though the ex-deputy exhibits a much sounder perspective on the fable than does the runner, his merely peripheral participation in the events of the episode itself, while perhaps appropriate to his position as a reader of the fable, may serve to represent an initial lack of capacity, if not of willingness, to see truth—particularly if one compares him to Sutterfield, that active participant who perceives truth in the fable two years before the ex-deputy does and who is one of the central characters not only in the horsethief episode but in *A Fable* as a whole. Sutterfield's responses to the variables in the situations in which he becomes involved demonstrate a refusal to adopt a rigid determination of right and wrong, as is evinced by his participation in the horse-rustling itself as well as by his toleration of the groom's gambling.

Sutterfield's remarks to the lawyer indicate the former's capacity to allow truth to emerge from the tale itself rather than imposing an inflexible code upon it and thereby distorting it for the sake of immediate apprehension. His primary concern centers on humanistic, not dogmatically theological, concerns—he does not even know if he has been ordained—and Faulkner implies that the tolerance imbedded in such a position serves both God and humanity better than, for example, the casuistry of the priest who interviews the Corporal. Sutterfield tells the lawyer: 'I bears witness. . . . To man. God dont need me.' When the lawyer responds that the 'most damning thing man could suffer would be a valid witness before God', Sutterfield corrects him: 'Man is full of sin and nature, and all he does dont bear looking at, and a heap of what he says is a shame and a mawkery. But cant no witness hurt him' (180). Sutterfield's credo as expressed in this passage would certainly be appropriate for an artist who, after all, bears witness to and for humanity. That such a vision should encompass all of human nature informs Sutterfield's remark to the runner:

> 'Evil is a part of man, evil and sin and cowardice, the same as repentance and being brave. You got to believe in all of them, or believe in none of them. Believe that man is capable of all of them, or he aint capable of none.' (203)

The runner misconstrues not only this statement but the fable as a whole, as appears in his proclamation that he will use the energy generated in him by the horsethief story 'to flee mankind for a little while' (203). While the sincerity of the runner's revivified idealism cannot be doubted, his 'conversion' becomes dangerous because, grounded in a partial understanding, it leads to fanaticism: he feels invulnerable, confident that although he may have to 'risk the rifle somewhere . . . it wouldn't matter where since it contained only (for him) one bullet while what he was armed with was capable of containing all of time, all of man' (209).

In the fervor of his beliefs, the runner very much resembles Nancy in *Requiem for a Nun*, which Faulkner wrote during a hiatus from his work on *A Fable*. The runner's actions, like Nancy's, are undertaken with the best of intentions but are often disastrous in their consequences and inconsistent with his professed creed. He sacrifices human life, for example, to support the idea that human life is sacred. Prior to the barrage, he not only disables five men while penetrating the lines to the front, but he also deliberately places in jeopardy the lives of Sutterfield, the sentry and indeed the whole battalion in order to affirm his principles. The runner's disguising himself and Sutterfield as figures of authority in order to pass through to the front casts a shadow on the integrity of the mission, especially since these disguises parallel those used by Lapin and Horse, the two criminals, in their attempt to reach Paris. Even in the terms of this rather sordid correspondence, the runner's deficiencies are apparent: like Lapin, he is the dominant figure; but unlike Lapin—who at least feels responsibility for Horse—the runner uses Sutterfield merely as a means to an end.

The runner's employing specious arguments to persuade the platoon to mutiny presents a more damning indictment. He seems as much a sophist as is Satan in *Paradise Lost* and *Paradise Regained*—two texts to which Faulkner alludes time and again in *A Fable*—admitting in private to Sutterfield that 'that's the risk: if some of the Germans do come out. Then they will shoot at us, both of them, their side and ours too—put a barrage down on all of us. They'll have to' (313), but never providing the platoon with this knowledge. Rather, he preys upon their xenophobia by intimating that the 'Senegalese and Moroccans and Kurds' (317) may consent to murder the others in the battalion just to end the war so that they can return to their native lands, and he dismisses the sentry's objections to the mutiny by attributing them to greed.

He then tells the platoon of the blank shells fired at the German airplane and insinuates that the ammunition on both sides remains blank.

The platoon accepts the runner's sophistry and follows its new leader's precedent by disposing of its officers. The irony of the runner's ultimately becoming the leader of the battalion hinges on his having rid himself of his commission in protest against his being invested with the power as an officer to 'tell vast herds of men what to do' (61) which is, of course, precisely what he now does. When the barrage comes, the runner continues to spout rhetoric, but in this instance it is that which he himself believes: 'They cant kill us! They cant! Not dare not: They cant!' (322). There is some truth in this outcry, insofar as the sacrifice of the two battalions can be seen as an affirmation of highest human aspirations; in another more immediate and practical sense, however, the runner is horribly wrong and the evidence of his error becomes strewn across the battlefield.

The barrage maims and disfigures the runner himself, and although he retains his indomitable spirit, his wounds emphasise the flaws in his perspective. The runner's outlook remains one-sided, and he becomes literally as well as symbolically only half a man, even though he continues unaware of his deficiencies in attitude to the end. At the conclusion of the novel, the runner paraphrases his final statement during the barrage, but with a crucial difference: rather than 'They cant kill us', he insists, 'I'm not going to die. Never'. The shift in pronouns epitomizes the runner's egocentrism. Were he speaking in the spiritual sense in the novel's conclusion, 'we' would be preferable. The sentry's use during the barrage of the plural personal pronoun indicates a sense of community, albeit brief, with his fellow men: ' "No!" he cried, "no! Not to us!" not even realising that he had said "we" and not "I" for the first time in his life probably, certainly for the first time in four years' (321). By contrast, the runner's use of the first person singular in his last remarks in *A Fable* implies that his entire 'spiritual' experience has been essentially a false epiphany.

It is not, of course, the runner who has the last word in *A Fable*. The Norman corrects someone's, perhaps the runner's, false impression by stating, 'I am not laughing. . . . What you see are tears'—this remark, and the conclusion as a whole, reflecting back to Sutterfield's comment that God has room for, and can grieve for, both laughter and tears. It seems appropriate that the Norman should be given the final remark in *A Fable* since he is a notable constructor of fables himself, most of them involving his grandiose estimation of the generalissimo. The Norman's reconstruction of the generalissimo's youth, like the tales of Sutpen developed by the various narrators in *Absalom, Absalom!* and those of the fliers offered by the reporter in *Pylon*, reveals as much about the fabulist as it does about the nominal subject of the fable.

The Norman's idealism links him with the other two members of that 'trinity of conscience' to which Faulkner so often referred in his remarks on *A Fable*:

> What I was writing about was the trilogy of man's conscience represented by the young British Pilot Officer, the Runner, and the Quartermaster General. The one that said, This is dreadful, terrible, and I won't face it even at the cost of my life—that was the British aviator. The [Quartermaster] General who said, This is terrible but we can bear it. The third one, the battalion Runner who said, This is dreadful, I won't stand it, I'll do something about it.[24]

Faulkner's placing of Levine, the Norman and the runner, respectively on an ascending scale of appropriate responses, however, pertains only insofar as the need to combat evil actively is concerned. *A Fable* as a whole demonstrates that the runner, like Starbuck in *Moby-Dick*—the novel Faulkner acknowledged as his model for the 'trinity of conscience'[25]—fails to contend with the full complexity of evil, his tendency toward oversimplification confounding the nobility of his intentions. Thus, the runner's flawed attempt to obliterate evil is both more laudable in its conception and more tragic in its consequences than, for example, the Norman's withdrawal.

One trait common to all three members of the 'trinity of conscience', and one that accords with their presentation as failed artist-figures, is that they all misuse language for the purpose of self-deception. The Norman, significantly enough, initially goes to Paris to be a painter but relinquishes his dream 'to the Military Academy for the sake of France' (254); although he abandons painting, his artistic inclinations and his idealism come to the fore, as does his misuse of language, in his appraisal of the generalissimo. He is the 'single classmate' who, when confronted with that negative legend of the generalissimo as a young man postulated by his other classmates, 'picked up the whole picture and reversed it' (253). The Norman's fertile imagination, feeding his 'passionate and hungry hope' (255), compels him to treat the generalissimo as a type of messiah. The Norman has done some reading—he is familiar with the Bible, with Byron, and, apparently, with one of Faulkner's own favorite books, *La Tentation de Saint Antoine*—and he attempts to match the generalissimo's actions with the enduring fables of the literature he has absorbed.

The Norman's persistent projection of the generalissimo as a messianic figure should nonetheless alert the reader to the Norman's extremist position. While not entirely mistaken, his partial view fails to account for the less favorable elements in the generalissimo's make-up. Consequently the Norman is shocked when he discovers that he has in part misread the generalissimo. The first blow to his illusions occurs as the story of the sacrifice of the homicidal soldier at the desert outpost is related by a countryman who, judging from his own tendency towards opulent expression, is something of a fabulist himself. The compatriot's recounting of the events in the desert, his insistence that the generalissimo be held liable for the man's death, and his suggestion that the generalissimo's behavior bears a demonic aspect—all serve to confront the Norman with a perspective on his messiah which he has never before entertained. This demonic fable functions, in fact, as a corrective to the Norman's messianic fable, just as the Norman's fable had 'reversed the picture' of previous fables.

This use of contradictory, corrective, or alternative fables constitutes one of the fundamental principles informing Faulkner's fiction: *Flags in the Dust, The Sound and the Fury, As I Lay Dying, Light in August, Pylon, Absalom, Absalom!, The Wild Palms, The Hamlet, Go Down, Moses,* and *Requiem for a Nun*—all rely in one way or another on the presentation of alternative fables which serve both to make the reader an active participant in the fictive process and to provide him with a comprehensive (and often composite) understanding of the situation. One might even speculate that all the novels function within the canon as such alternative fables, treating the eternal themes of literature from radically different perspectives and precisely by means of their opposition imbuing the canon with that 'design' which Faulkner asserted was requisite to the entire body of an author's work.[26] The varied fables of *A Fable,* like those that comprise the canon as a whole, assert the complexity of experience and choice, imply the possibility of a seemingly infinite number of different interpretations, and insist on the reader's holding in suspension those oppositions which so distinctively characterize Faulkner's work.

Just prior to the description of the Norman's response to the alternative fable related at the sanatorium, in which the Norman tries to excuse his hero by virtue of the generalissimo's youth at the time of the episode in the desert, Faulkner inserts a brief passage describing the moment, twenty-five years in the future, when the generalissimo would offer the Norman the appointment of Quartermaster General. In the next episode in which the Norman plays a significant role, he tries to resign from that appointment. Apparently having learned nothing from the sanatorium fable, the Norman has remained in the intervening period just as he was then: 'indomitable . . . obdurate, incurable and doomed with hope' (271). Like the runner, he remains self-deluded, and similar to the runner's progressively deteriorating physical condition, the Norman's persistent illness functions as a metaphor for a spiritual and imaginative malaise. The misconceived belief upon which his hope is based 'dooms' him, Faulkner suggesting that although, as the ex-deputy comes to realize, 'truth [is] truth' (159), only by recognizing the myriad elements which comprise truth can one escape a recurrent cycle of artificially buoyed hope and crushing disillusionment.

In his fervent desire to shape the generalissimo into the character he would like him to be, the Norman excuses or ignores the negative aspects of the generalissimo's nature; he cannot, however, blind himself to the evil inherent in the barrage, after which he tries to resign his position and so retroactively repudiate his responsibility for the massacre. Like the numerous other attempts at resignation in *A Fable*, the Norman's represents a betrayal of his duties as character, reader, and fabulist. The generalissimo punctures the Norman's attitude of righteous indignation and recalls him to his duties by revealing that the Corporal was betrayed by one of his own disciples, thereby indicating that no single group has a monopoly on evil. The generalissimo then contrasts the Norman's 'bitter self-flagellation' (332) and tacit martyr-complex with the upcoming genuine sacrifice of the Corporal which the Corporal himself will accept with equanimity. Defeated, the Norman begins to leave until the generalissimo reminds him that he has forgotten his 'paper' of resignation. The Norman responds 'Yes . . . . So I did' (332).

This innocuous reply later assumes much significance in that these words are almost identical with those used by the priest when the Corporal reminds him that he has forgotten his 'gear'—signifying the responsibilities of the priest's own office—after their interview (367). Like the Norman, the priest has been profoundly disillusioned by his encounter with reality, but the result differs markedly in the two instances: the priest commits suicide; the Norman endures. These differing responses imply that, despite the pervasive presence of evil, the retention of some type of hope in mankind—however partial or misguided the basis for that hope might be—better equips one to adapt to life's vicissitudes. The Norman becomes disillusioned when he finds reason to despair; the priest destroys himself when he finds reason to hope. Despite the Norman's failings, the very fact of his endurance compels some degree of admiration. His will to continue is emphasized by Faulkner's placing the story of his attempted resignation immediately following the account of Levine's suicide.

Like the Norman and the runner, Levine's idealism shatters upon a confrontation with evil; unlike the other two, however, his reaction is not willed endurance but self-destruction. As with the Norman and the runner, Levine's idealism reflects the quality of understanding he brings to his reading: despite the relatively short time that he spends in the battle zone, he becomes known throughout the squadron as an inveterate reader. Yet he too lacks the perception to determine genuine significance in the material which he reads, to go beyond reducing the truths presented in it to a simple dichotomy of good and evil. Such a reduction accounts for both his vainglorious conception of war in general and the letter to his mother which he plans to write and then plant among his belongings: 'the succinct and restrained and modestly heroic one' (91) he envisions being sent home after his glorious death defending king and country. Clearly, Levine also self-consciously creates fictions and, like other fabulists in *A Fable*, the value of his fiction suffers from the simplistic, polarized view upon which it feeds.

During the crisis created by the short armistice, Levine reads Walter Pater's *Gaston de Latour*, set in the reign of Charles IX when religious wars were devastating France. In *Gaston*, interestingly enough, Pater comments upon a temporary armistice which occurs in the midst of the wars; more importantly, perhaps, numerous passages indicate that the causes of war are various and that self-interest plays at least as important a role in the conflict as does religious zeal. The complexity of motivation in war provides a lesson which Levine would have done well to note, but he fails to do so.

As with Gragnon's reading of *Gil Blas*, Faulkner uses the central character in Pater's novel to counterpoint Levine's failure, the young airman's misreading of the text thereby forming another cautionary example for the reader of *A Fable* and of Faulkner in general. Like Levine, Gaston comes into maturity at a time of cultural and social upheaval: born into the age of the Renaissance, he confronts a milieu in which time-honored ideas are being challenged. When his vision of a world in which absolute good opposes absolute evil is undermined, Gaston finds it extraordinarily difficult to accommodate experiences which reveal his perspective to be inadequate. Yet adapt he does, surviving even the tremendous shock of the St Bartholomew's Day Massacre. One source of Gaston's ability to assimilate a recognition of evil stems from the time he spends with Montaigne. Unlike Levine, Gaston learns from his study of the masters, and although the 'romance' was left incomplete, Pater evidently thought of Gaston as a survivor.

Levine, on the other hand, can come to terms with neither peace nor war because both fail to conform to his idealistic preconceptions. When the German general shoots his pilot, for example, Levine is utterly confused: outraged initially because the Allies violate the rules of warfare in allowing an enemy general safe passage to their side, he becomes equally aghast when the German general acts in strict accordance with those rules in executing his pilot for landing an undamaged plane behind enemy lines. Bewildered by events which do not correspond to the rules of conduct he has embraced and even formulated, Levine responds to what he finds to be an incomprehensible world by retreating ever more deeply into solipsism—a solipsism which, significantly enough in terms of his status as an artist-figure, tends to equate world with word.

Even after Levine becomes determined to commit suicide, he abandons neither his inadequate ideals nor their source, continuing to indulge in 'some of the reading he had imagined himself doing between patrols—the hero living by proxy the lives of heroes between the monotonous peaks of his own heroic derring' (324). When Bridesman, whose very name suggests a passage into maturity, explains the reasons for the barrage, Levine finds in the explanation merely a confirmation of his perception of unfathomable yet palpable evil; as a consequence, he calmly carries out his plan of avoiding being contaminated by that evil by destroying himself.

The priest who interviews the Corporal in the same chapter chooses, like Levine, to commit suicide, but for different reasons: a cynic rather than an idealist, the priest holds no brief for 'furious and intractable dreamers' (363). Judging from his misconstruction of the passages he cites from the New Testament, however, he strongly resembles Levine in his inability, or refusal, to comprehend the truths in literary and religious fables; the priest is perhaps the most explicit example in *A Fable* of the reader who distorts his reading in order to make it coincide with his predetermined beliefs. Incontrovertibly earthbound, the priest even 'corrects' Christ who, he insists, failed to 'realise the true significance of what He was saying' because He believed that 'He was speaking poetic metaphor, synonym, parable' (364) when actually He was speaking literally. This assertion runs directly contrary to Faulkner's implicit contention in *A Fable*, made explicit elsewhere, that truth lies not in the facts or the circumstances of fable and myth but in the spirit conveyed by these 'matchless allegories'. Those like the priest misconstrue the meaning and purpose of such fables by reading them literally and exploiting them for the purpose of supporting their own misguided attitudes.

That the priest's devotion pertains more directly to the mundane than to the spiritual and the imaginative appears in his twice beginning to quote Christ as to rendering unto Caesar the things which are Caesar's without ever reaching the statement's crucial conclusion: 'And unto God the things which are God's'. Analogously, he misconstrues Christ's assertion that 'Man does not live by bread alone', making a minor error in the quotation—an ominous sign in itself—and then interpreting it not as a recognition of, and promise to provide for, the human need of spiritual sustenance, but as a condemnation of what the generalissimo terms human passion for 'unfact'. The priest's being an emissary from the generalissimo consolidates one's sense of his having betrayed the obligations of his office. And his gloss of Satan's tempting Christ to throw himself from the parapet—anticipating the later interview between the generalissimo and the Corporal—further reveals his failings as a theologian and as a human being: he asserts that it constitutes a temptation to 'immortality' (365), rather than to presumption. Ironically enough, he himself shortly thereafter yields to a variant of this temptation by 'cast[ing] himself sideways and downward' (370) upon the bayonet, and as a consequence rendering himself guilty of presumption, not only in his mimicry of the lance piercing Christ's side, but in his bland assurance that *'He will forgive me'* (370). The priest's request just prior to his suicide that the Corporal read to him the office for the dying indicates his own deficiencies as an interpreter of the eternal truths as well as his ultimate acceptance of the Corporal's superior capacities as priest.

The Corporal is, however, illiterate, Faulkner thereby suggesting that there are those who have an intuitive apprehension of the verities, who can 'read' the intricacies and ramifications of the fables of life without the need of external reference—a mode of understanding which he develops explicitly in the presentation of both the Corporal and his sister, Marya. She and her sister, Marthe, become involved as children in trying to piece together, and interpret the meaning of, their mother's relationship with the generalissimo; Marthe tells the generalissimo in the interview at Chaulnesmont: 'we only watched and saw and knitted, knotted, tried to, what simple threads we had of implication' (289). The reconstruction which Marthe goes on to detail would thus seem to be the product of a collaborative effort by her and Marya; it becomes apparent in the course of the interview, however, that the interpretation is primarily Marthe's. Her 'demonizing' of the generalissimo recalls Rosa's remarks on Thomas Sutpen in *Absalom, Absalom!*, displaying a rhetoric fraught with the same urgency, frustration, grief, and malice.

Marya's attitude towards the generalissimo differs significantly, for she evinces an immediate, intuitive, appreciation of his position: 'I'm glad to see you anyway . . . . You look so exactly like what you are. . . . You really cant help [what you are], can you? You really cant' (284). This assessment anticipates the Norman's remark to the generalissimo during the course of his loquacious attempt to resign: '[You] did not even what you would but what you must, since you are you' (328). Unlike the Norman, however, Marya entertains no illusions concerning human capacity for both good and evil.

Although described at one point as having 'the peaceful face of the witless' (214), Marya is no Benjy Compson. Her apparent responsibility for the 'miracles' of the basket and the spoon manifests the power underlying her serenity, while her rapport with the generalissimo and her numerous affinities with the Corporal suggest that, like them, she intuitively understands and accepts the intricacies of motivation and response which confound so many of the other characters. She certainly has a more profound comprehension of the meaning of the fable as a whole than does Marthe, a contrast nowhere more evident than when the runner and Polchek (the Judas figure) visit the farmhouse. As the two men are coming up the lane Marya tells her sister, 'one is looking for a tree' (426), thus indicating her foreknowledge of Polchek's eventual suicide; she also recognizes Polchek's Zsettlani heritage, which initially escapes her sister. In fact, in many respects she seems to know both Polchek and the runner better than they know themselves.

In the farmhouse episode, Faulkner emphasises again and again that the runner keeps his eye trained on Marthe rather than on Marya, thus underscoring the runner's superficial conception of the message which he chooses to carry. Entranced by Marthe because she looks so much like the Corporal, he ignores Marya even though she more nearly embodies, on whatever reductive level, the essence of those qualities which the Corporal dies to defend: honour, courage, humility, pride and compassion. Marya, on the other hand, understands the runner thoroughly, interpreting favorably his '*Consummatum est*'—'He's finished' (431)—declaration with reference to the Corporal and recognizing his love of laughter; only when they join in this release does the runner's eye briefly meet hers. With typical prescience, she anticipates the conclusion of the fable by telling Marthe that the runner 'can move fast enough. He will be there in plenty of time' (431–2). Marya also resembles the Corporal in her capacity to accept without condemnation everyone with whom she comes in contact, including the generalissimo directly responsible for her brother's execution.

It is, of course, most difficult for the reader to arrive at any clear estimation of the generalissimo, since Faulkner undoubtedly designed him as an elusive and enigmatic figure, somewhat akin to other Faulknerian 'absent centers' such as Caddy, Addie, Sutpen and, indeed, the Corporal, around whom the action of a given text revolves. The generalissimo seems at one and the same time to be both God and Satan, to incarnate both the heights of human aspiration and the depths of human corruption. *A Fable*'s insistence that all people are composed of elements of good and evil reaches its greatest intensification in the generalissimo. He seems not so much to have resolved the enigma of the human condition as to have accepted and embodied it, thereby remaining free of the self-torture and self-delusion so prominent in many of the other characters. His ability to recognize and hold in suspension the relative merits of both his own and the Corporal's position casts him, in a sense, in the role of ideal reader, and he seems also to be in many respects the ultimate artist-figure in *A Fable*: extremely intelligent, apparently omniscient, omnipotent in the spheres in which he operates, and not only aware of the ramifications of the fable in which he is involved but capable, to a certain extent, of orchestrating it. Although he keeps only military manuals in his personal quarters, his interview with the Corporal demonstrates a close familiarity with some of the classic literary works as well. His familiarity with the New Testament fable which serves as the scenario for *A Fable*, the original 'text', is everywhere apparent.

The characterization of the generalissimo seems to derive in part from familiar literary figures as well. In his role as Supreme Commander of the Allied forces, his motto could well be that of Andrew Undershaft in George Bernard Shaw's *Major Barbara*—'Unashamed'. Indeed, the parallels go further: Undershaft owns a huge munitions factory, a position which he, as an orphan, inherited from the previous owner. The generalissimo is likewise an orphan and the godson of a munitions maker. Undershaft has a son named Stephen, whom he abandons; the generalissimo has a bastard son, Stefan, whom he forsakes as well. Cusins repeatedly refers to Undershaft as 'Mephistopheles', partly because the latter fully recognizes man's capacity for base behavior and entertains no illusions concerning the possibility of establishing a permanent peace. Certain attitudes of the generalissimo seem similarly Mephistophelean and, like Undershaft, he remains free of illusion, as is evident in the description of him given early in the novel:

> the slight gray man with a face wise, intelligent, and unbelieving, who no longer believed in anything but his disillusion and his intelligence and his limitless power. (13)

Taking into consideration the detrimental effects which the shattering of illusion has on other characters in *A Fable*, the generalissimo's serene acceptance of his disillusionment need not necessarily be considered negative.

The ambiguity of the description does, however, typify the aura of mystery surrounding the generalissimo, much of it the consequence of the reader's information about him coming from second-hand sources, such as the Norman and Marthe, all of whom remain unreliable because their reports quite evidently stem from imaginative reconstruction filtered through personal bias. By keeping the generalissimo a shadowy figure, Faulkner implicitly invites the reader of *A Fable* to 'knit' and 'knot' the relevant 'threads of implication' (289) concerning the character's behavior, attitudes and past life into an independent fable. Even when the generalissimo himself enters directly into the narrative, the enigma—no doubt by design—is compounded rather than resolved. Nor do Faulkner's public statements provide any easy solution to the puzzle. He habitually referred to the generalissimo in terms of the character's demonic traits, but even in that vein his remarks seem to have contained as much praise as condemnation:

> Well, to me he was the dark, splendid, fallen angel. The good shining cherubim to me are not very interesting, it's the dark, gallant, fallen one that is moving to me.[27]

While Faulkner's comments on the generalissimo quite deliberately deny a pat formulation of the character's role, references made in other contexts support the view that he in some sense represents an artist. On a variety of occasions Faulkner metaphorically associated the 'dark, gallant, fallen one'—Satan—with the creative impulse. For instance, in an address delivered at Pine Manor Junior College on 8 June 1953, at which time Faulkner was still working on *A Fable*, he referred to 'the philosophers and artists, the articulate and grieving who have reminded us always of our capacity for honour and courage and compassion and pity and sacrifice' as being 'avatars of [Satan's] rebellious and uncompromising pride'.[28] Faulkner's close association of the materials in *A Fable* and those in the Pine Manor address may be further indicated by the fact that some of the versos of the typescript setting copy for the novel contain drafts of the address.[29]

Faulkner's references to poets and philosophers as possessing some of Satan's characteristics seem almost to be echoing Blake's assertion that:

> The reason Milton wrote in fetters when he wrote of Angels & God, and at liberty when of Devils & Hell, is because he was a true Poet and of the Devil's party without knowing it.[30]

In *A Fable*, certainly, Faulkner quite elaborately gives this devil his due, most notably when the generalissimo 'tempts' his son on the hill overlooking Chaulnesmont. As the generalissimo has previously told the Norman, the interview's result is a foregone conclusion. The generalissimo nevertheless insists upon it not only for personal reasons but also, apparently, to provide the 'passion play' which he has dominated with its climactic scene. His remarks on the hilltop evoke God, Satan and Caesar, while his son's laconicism recalls Milton's Christ in *Paradise Regained*. Millgate has suggested that it is possible to read this interview as a 'dramatic externalization of a conflict that might be conceived of as existing within the mind of a single person'.[31] That person could well be an artist, for, among other things, Faulkner in this passage wrestles with the same angel—or devil, as the case may be—with whom he grappled in such early writings as 'The Artist' and 'Carcassonne'. Throughout the episode he deals once again with the irresolvable conflict between the imagination which aspires and the earth which contains. Both are necessary to the artist: the former, which the Corporal embodies, for inspiration; the latter, which the generalissimo defends, for material. Faulkner treats these two representatives of the poles of the opposition without apparent bias: the generalissimo and the Corporal respect one another's position, and the reader should do no less. The generalissimo succinctly defines the relative positions of the Corporal and himself:

> 'we are two articulations, self-elected possibly, anyway elected, anyway postulated, not so much to defend as to test two inimical conditions which, through no fault of ours but through the simple paucity and restrictions of the arena where they meet, must contend and—one of them—perish: I champion of this mundane earth which, whether I like it or not, is, and to which I did not ask to come, yet since I am here, not only must stop but intend to stop during my allotted while; you champion

of an esoteric realm of man's baseless hopes and his infinite capacity—no: passion—for unfact.' (347–8)

The generalissimo's categorization of himself and the Corporal as 'articulations' serves to emphasise once again the fictive, fabular nature of *A Fable*. His reiteration of much of Faulkner's Nobel Prize speech in the course of the 'temptation' reinforces his presentation as an artist and may be attributed to his recognition of the human need for some type of spiritual fulfillment; his son, simply to stay in character, must remain much more reticent. This does not, of course, suggest that the generalissimo is the moral exemplar in *A Fable*, many of his actions being, after all, diabolical in the strict sense of the term. Yet he and the Corporal, taken together, signify the writer's grief, sacrifice and ultimate triumph, both finally succeeding within the limitations of their respective spheres. The generalissimo provides for the 'whole Western world' the 'right and privilege to mourn in peace without terror or concern' (433), and, although double-edged, this evaluation of his accomplishment does suggest at least a partial fulfillment of his 'mission'. The spirit incarnated in the Corporal will live on through the eleven themselves—who, as the generalissimo recognizes, will be 'witnesses to all the earth' (347).

In *A Fable*, Faulkner himself bears witness to humanity, to the quickened dust compounded of variant measures of good and evil. There are some indications that at times during the composition of *A Fable* he may have intended it to be his last book, that he thought of it in certain respects as his *Tempest*, after the completion of which he could, in an action evocative of Prospero's disposal of his staff, 'break the pencil and cast it all away'.[32] Indeed, much of the magic and mystery so predominant in *A Fable* may stem precisely from such an association. Prospero's position as an artist-figure becomes virtually self-evident in Shakespeare's play; in *A Fable* the numerous artist-figures, most of whom either fail as fabulists or achieve only a very limited success, serve to register indirectly both Faulkner's high standards and his achievement. Faulkner's implicitly encouraging the reader of *A Fable* to 'knit' and 'knot' those relevant 'threads of implication' (289) into his own fable describes a process equally necessary to arriving at an understanding of each of the individual novels and, indeed, of their relation one to another within the canon. Although Faulkner's revels would not in fact end until eight years after the publication of *A Fable,* it seems fitting that a writer so misunderstood during the course of his career should incorporate into his '*magnum opus*' a series of fables which not only suggest to the reader a mode of interpreting *A Fable* itself, but also provide a means of access to the understanding of the entire canon.

7

Conclusion

The network of fables interwoven to make up *A Fable*—indeed, the very choice of title for what Faulkner saw as so cumulative and culminating a work—indirectly signals to the reader the potentially fabular aspects of Faulkner's other writings. If, however, each of his novels may be read as a fable, he seems to have reserved his most overtly fabular effects for the non-Yoknapatawpha novels. The anonymity of so many of the key characters in the final three non-Yoknapatawpha works serves to imbue each of them with a potential 'everyman' or, as in the case of the reporter and the convict, 'no man' function, while the obviously symbolic connotations of the names assigned to specifically identified characters throughout the non-Yoknapatawpha fiction clearly enhance the fabular qualities of these novels as a group. In one way or another, all five novels constitute fables of creativity appertaining not only to art and the artist but also to the reader and the reader's responsibilities to the text. That the two pre-Yoknapatawpha novels, *Soldiers' Pay* and *Mosquitoes*, should concern themselves with such issues manifests Faulkner's uncertainty about the direction his work should take prior to his decision to explore his own 'little postage stamp of native soil'. On the other hand, Faulkner used the three purely non-Yoknapatawpha novels both to experiment with narrative, stylistic and structural techniques before incorporating them into the Yoknapatawpha fiction and to provide the reader with keys to a body of work which was still being so grossly misunderstood.

Pylon, for example, anticipates *Absalom, Absalom!* not only in the intensity of its stylistic expression but also in the reporter's being an unreliable narrator whose personal biases prevent him from making the story he tells entirely credible. As with the four narrators in *Absalom, Absalom!*, the focus of attention in *Pylon* is not so much on the putative subjects of the tale as on the teller: just as each successive version of the Sutpen story modifies and alters the previous versions without necessarily superseding them, so do the reporter's two distinctive perspectives on the fliers exist in an antagonistic symbiosis, their related though opposite forms of extremism subverting, at least with regard to the reporter, the process of narration itself. If, however, the polarities which inform the reporter's attitude in *Pylon* serve to emphasise the possibility of using language to distort meaning, the contrast between the taciturn convict and the loquacious Harry in *The Wild Palms* affirms the value of 'thinking it into words', of employing language in order to attain an integrated perspective. The structure of *The Wild Palms* insists on the separateness of the two stories and at the same time on their status as a single novel, underscoring both the difficulty of achieving such an integration and the necessity of doing so, and thereby placing emphasis upon the recognition of the interplay of oppositions as a prime component in the discovery of truth.

The deliberate divergence of 'Wild Palms' and 'Old Man' stresses that the dynamic of juxtaposition which forms so prominent a feature of Faulkner's narrative strategy in general represents an ongoing process, spanning gaps of time and place—not a Hegelian dialectic, to be sure, since Faulkner resists synthesis and resolution, but one in which the meaning lies in the persistent friction of irreconcilables rather than in their fusion. Indeed, *The Wild Palms* may even be read as the fictional embodiment of an approach to the canon as a whole, the distinctions between 'Wild Palms' and 'Old Man' implicitly asserting the possibility of reading each text in the canon as an independent fiction, even as the correlations between the two fables no less insistently reflect the value of moving beyond such readings to a comprehensive overview. The adjustments which the reader must make in respect of the separate stories while registering the divergencies and correspondences between 'Wild Palms' and 'Old Man' and noting the way in which a reading of each chapter influences the response to every other chapter—these mirror the modifications that must be made when moving among the different novels in the canon, whether in chronological order or not. Since the action in 'Wild Palms' for the most part takes place outside of Mississippi while 'Old Man' uses Mississippi as its major setting, Faulkner's joining of the two in a single novel serves to demonstrate the fundamental interrelationship of all his works and especially the importance of the non-Yoknapatawpha fiction in any comprehensive assessment of the canon—an implication supported within the individual stories by the Mississippi convict's journeying to areas beyond the state lines and by Harry and Charlotte's odyssey terminating in Mississippi.

A high concentration of movement from place to place presents an element common to all of the non-Yoknapatawpha novels, the wanderlust of the characters serving to some extent as a correlative for social displacement. Yet in keeping with the fact that in the non-Yoknapatawpha novels Faulkner was himself moving beyond the borders of his fictional county, those characters who travel the farthest in these novels—Joe Gilligan, David West, Harry Wilbourne and Tobe Sutterfield spring immediately to mind—tend to gain the most penetrating insights into themselves and others, often achieving a stability denied to those who fear to venture outside of their own regions.[1] These five texts in effect serve to establish a relationship between Faulkner's imaginative county and the world at large—a relationship also implicit in his allowing his Yoknapatawpha characters on occasion to roam to such 'alien' locales as Memphis and New York. In the non-Yoknapatawpha novels, Faulkner was giving exclusive emphasis to regions beyond the geographical area with which he was most familiar and at the same time experimenting with 'uncharted' narrative techniques—delving in a double sense into somewhat unfamiliar terrain. These forays thus correspond to Faulkner's insistence on the artist's continually experimenting with his craft. At the same time, their settings not only demonstrate that the central concerns of his work are universal but also provide a quality of counterpoint for the canon comparable to that found within each of the individual novels.

Just as 'Old Man' serves as foil to 'Wild Palms', so can the horsethief episode in *A Fable*—part of which, like the crucial 'alligator hunting' interlude in 'Old Man', takes place in Cajun country—be read as the formulation of a different, and often opposite, perspective on themes and incidents analogous to those in the central narrative. In the horsethief episode, for example, the active rebellion against authority of the townspeople arises from the basest of prejudices—they do not approve of 'rich niggers' being within the city limits—but brings about the favorable consequence of Sutterfield's release; in the central narrative, however, the passive rebellion of Gragnon's division originates in laudable intentions but ultimately leads to wholesale slaughter and remains negligible in effect. Again, the deputy sheriff in Missouri in a socially impotent authority figure who intends to whisk Sutterfield off to a nearby town in order to save him, whereas the omnipotent generalissimo (whose chauffeur bears a striking resemblance to the driver of the 'getaway car' in the horsethief episode) takes the Corporal to the hill overlooking Chaulnesmont for the purpose of affirming his doom. The horsethief episode can thus be identified as the chief among that series of fables in *A Fable* in which the alteration and alternation of perspective contributes to the exhaustive treatment of the thematic concerns at the core of the novel itself, and at the same time expands outward to instruct the reader's apprehension of relationships among those fables comprising the canon.

The fables in Faulkner's non-Yoknapatawpha fiction tend by their sheer profusion and opposition to deny the possibility of drawing a clear and distinct moral; or rather they demonstrate that the moral lies not so much in the tales themselves as in their discrete and divergent tellings, one of which should be the reader's own. Faulkner's narrative strategies imply rather than prescribe, reveal rather than define, and that refusal of closure so common in the non-Yoknapatawpha novels ensures that the reader, in a manner resembling that of the characters in each text, will actively participate in the dual processes of reading and re-presenting these fables. The very number of readers within the non-Yoknapatawpha fiction testifies to Faulkner's concern with the quality of perception that will be brought to bear by his own 'external' readers, and the failure of so many of these characters to 'read' accurately the situations in which they become involved serves to warn the reader of the text about the pitfalls of distorting literature in order to make it coincide with prejudice or support illusion.

The varying abilities of the readers presented in the non-Yoknapatawpha fiction often suggest a correlation between their respective capacities for sympathetic understanding of literature and their potential for coming to terms with life itself. The strengths and weaknesses of both Gilligan and Jones in *Soldiers' Pay* appear in their differing attitudes towards, and aptitudes for, their reading. In *Mosquitoes*, while Fairchild's defense of modern poetry relates to his benevolent attitude in other respects, it also manifests his penchant for theorizing about literature, whereas Ayers's unsophisticated attempt to come to terms with specific poems not only represents the layman's perspective but also contrasts favorably with, for example, Mark Frost's gnomisms. The reporter in *Pylon* compulsively reads that most ephemeral of literary by-products, the newspaper, and thereby accrues to himself all of the negative connotations associated with newsprint throughout the novel, ultimately appearing to be as insubstantial personally as the medium to which he is devoted. While the convict's criticisms of pulp literature in *The Wild Palms* reflect that sub-genre's infidelity to life, his continuing to devour third-rate literature even after it has led him into folly illustrates his blindness to his own defects, indicates that he refuses to learn from experience, and betrays the puerile romanticism hidden beneath his hard-boiled exterior.

Gragnon and Levine in *A Fable* embody diametrically opposite approaches to literature, the former exhibiting a grave suspicion of any work of the imagination, the latter delving into it wholeheartedly at every opportunity. Their reading also affects them in different ways: Gragnon, displaying an attitude analogous to that of the convict in *The Wild Palms,* assumes fiction to be reality; Levine, on the other hand, expects reality to conform to fiction. Although different, the two attitudes are equally misguided, Gragnon's underscoring the utter lack of imagination and flexibility which precipitates his downfall, Levine's signalling the idealism and inability to adjust to disruptions in preconceived patterns which lead to his suicide. In contrast to both, Gragnon's aide extracts truths from literature without codifying them into rigid rules of behavior, and his death accordingly attains an aura of nobility and a sense of purpose lacking in the inconsequential deaths of Gragnon and Levine. While it may seem peculiar that two of the most perceptive 'readers' of the situation in *A Fable,* Sutterfield and the Corporal, are illiterate, their being so serves to reflect Faulkner's apparent belief that attitude and approach figure as importantly as does breadth of knowledge in determining one's capacities as a reader. The ideal reader would, of course, combine the best of both disposition and depth and thus be able to distinguish the essential without becoming blinded either to subtleties or to broad patterns of meaning. In *A Fable,* the generalissimo, although certainly not an entirely sympathetic character, comes closest to exhibiting these traits. He remains throughout aware of the mythic overtones of the fable and capable of accepting and enduring those oppositions which torture so many of the others in *A Fable* and in the canon in general.

At the time that he was writing the last three non-Yoknapatawpha novels, Faulkner must have recognized the acute need for just such an ideal reader of his own works, and part of the purpose of these three novels may have been to supply a corrective to misconceptions current among contemporary appraisals of his work—or, if not for the benefit of contemporary commentators, then for posterity's sake. One such misconception which the later non-Yoknapatawpha fiction clearly undercuts is that of Faulkner as an untutored backwoods genius unfamiliar with any literature but his own and isolated from the main currents of his times. *Pylon, The Wild Palms* and *A Fable* teem with allusions of all sorts, direct and indirect reference being made not only to literary texts but also to biblical, mythological, and even, on rare occasions, philosophical sources,[2] and it seems reasonable to speculate that Faulkner may have intended, in so doing, to draw attention to the presence of more deeply imbedded allusions within the Yoknapatawpha fiction.

In *The Wild Palms,* as we have seen, he was at one level deeply concerned to confront the challenge presented in the success of his contemporary Ernest Hemingway, much as he had, in effect, 'taken on' John Dos Passos in the pages of *Pylon*. This is not necessarily to suggest that Faulkner was bitter about the praise and profit accorded to contemporary authors at a time when his own works were going out of print: Faulkner always had a confident, and accurate, estimation of his own merits as a writer. Rather, the more generous—and perhaps more plausible—view would hold that since, like the other non-Yoknapatawpha novels, *Pylon* and *The Wild Palms* constitute fables of creativity, cautionary tales concerning art and the artist, it could well be that in the Dos Passos and Hemingway correspondences and inversions Faulkner was assserting the need for every writer to abandon familiar patterns and models, even his own, in order to ensure the integrity of his craft and the vitality of his work.

It is notable that all of the first four non-Yoknapatawpha novels—*Soldiers' Pay* and *Mosquitoes* as well as *Pylon* and *The Wild Palms*—are deliberately and specifically contemporaneous, seeming to derive from and speak to the forms and issues characteristic of the fiction of their day and even to some of their author's most recent experiences. While the 'war setting' of *A Fable* may render it topical in a general sense, however, the novel does appear to be deliberately displaced both in time and in space from the immediate social context of its composition. Published in 1954, it is set during the latter part of the First World War, and in its pages Faulkner stresses the mythic, essentially timeless, aspects of the great conflict. Yet it is conceivable that the distinctly fabular qualities of *A Fable* were prompted in part by Faulkner's memory of the novels that followed the First World War and so embodied an anticipatory reaction—a pre-emptive strike—against the spate of war novels likely to be published after the Second World War had come to an end. He began work on the novel in 1943, and although he was not to complete it until approximately ten years had passed, its basic outline seems to have been present in his mind from a very early stage and to have corresponded, broadly speaking, to the much later statement, possibly prepared for the dust-jacket of the first edition, in which he emphasised that *A Fable* was not an anti-war novel.[3]

The relationship between *A Fable* and *Soldiers' Pay* resembles in some respects that between *The Wild Palms* and *Mosquitoes*, Faulkner in each instance exploring similar themes in the later novel from a more mature perspective and thereby indirectly providing an internal justification for investigating the non-Yoknapatawpha novels as a group. Indeed, he may have had his earlier novel about the aftermath of the First World War quite specifically in mind as he wrote *A Fable*, the muted despair prevalent in the former being counterpointed by the qualified optimism of the latter. These two works, the first and the last of the non-Yoknapatawpha novels, also resemble each other in being the most evidently allusive and formally stylized of any of Faulkner's works, the far greater adroitness in integrating allusions and deploying formal techniques in *A Fable* showing how far Faulkner had developed in his transition from 'apprentice' to 'master'. Ultimately, his refusal in *A Fable* to align himself explicitly with the course of contemporary fiction assumes as much significance for the reader of the canon as does his earlier fidelity to prevailing attitudes and modes of expression in *Soldiers' Pay*.

A Fable seems somewhat anomalous in a consideration of the non-Yoknapatawpha novels as a group not only by virtue of its resolute avoidance of contemporaneity but also because it appears to possess—apart from brief personal references in the presentation of Levine and Conventicle—far fewer autobiographical elements than any of the other four novels. In *A Fable*, this approach serves the purpose of virtually excluding from the mythic ambience any tincture of personal reminscence or anecdote, Faulkner perhaps having decided that the authors of all lasting myths—or, more appropriately, the composite author of the one great fable which is world literature—should remain anonymous in principle, even if not in fact. In interviews, Faulkner consistently downplayed the importance of the author as an individual, instead placing emphasis on the text itself. For example, in the *Paris Review* interview Faulkner commented:

> If I had not existed, someone else would have written me, Hemingway, Dostoevsky, all of us. Proof of that is that there are about three candidates for the authorship of Shakespeare's plays. But what is important is *Hamlet* and *Midsummer Night's Dream*, not who wrote them, but that somebody did. The artist is of no importance. Only what he creates is important.[4]

Actually, it might well be that the true anomaly lies not in the absence of personal references from *A Fable* but in their unusually obtrusive presence, in one form or another, in the other four non-Yoknapatawpha novels—which are, after all, designedly distanced from the region in which Faulkner lived and upon which he set his literary imprint.

The autobiographical aspects of *Soldiers' Pay* and *Mosquitoes* may be attributable to the young Faulkner's relying heavily on his own experiences while polishing his craft. It is notable, however, that even in these 'notes toward a supreme fiction' he was exhibiting tendencies in his incorporation of autobiographical material which would carry over into his mature work. One such tendency consists in his ironic treatment of such figures as Januarius Jones, Mark Frost, and even the character in *Mosquitoes* named Faulkner, all of whom exhibit some of their author's own personal traits. That each of these sardonically-conceived figures is nevertheless a fledgling writer may suggest that Faulkner's carefully disengaged engagement with them may be one aspect of his attempts during his apprenticeship period to discover his own literary persona.

This implicit quest takes on other forms in the later non-Yoknapatawpha novels, especially in terms of Faulkner's creation of the characters through whom he pursues a determination of the qualities necessary to the preservation of artistic integrity. Although *Pylon*, like *Mosquitoes*, derives much of its detail from Faulkner's experiences, none of its characters seem even remotely associated with him. The reporter's deficiencies as an author do, however, provide a splendid example of how *not* to approach a subject in fiction. His dual problem of remaining too distant from the fliers (his characters) and becoming overly involved with them may relate to those problems with *Absalom, Absalom!* which the writing of *Pylon* apparently helped Faulkner to resolve. Similarly, the fact that the two stories in *The Wild Palms* present diverse fables of the artist to some extent implicates Faulkner himself in each. The convict's comic capitulation to his desire for security obversely indicates Faulkner's commitment to experimentalism as essential to artistic growth. And if Harry's acceptance of grief reflects Faulkner's basically tragic view of life, that same character's fundamentally artistic affirmation demonstrates one way in which the artist may use such grief to triumph over despair. The many artist-figures in *A Fable* verify the extent to which it too is a fable of creativity, concentrating not so much on the war or on the Christian analogue as upon the narrative impulse underlying the creation of all fables, and presenting varied examples of the ways in which the teller can shape the tale to produce meaning, distort material to satisfy personal compulsions, or shirk the responsibilities of narration altogether.

In a sense, every story implicates the author, and certainly Faulkner is present in the Yoknapatawpha novels as well. Yet his presence in those works seems in general to be more muted and submerged than in those set outside Yoknapatawpha. It is, indeed, possible that Faulkner tended to avoid the incorporation of overt personal references into the Yoknapatawpha works precisely in order to emphasise that they were fictions, not disguised autobiography. There was little danger of such a misinterpretation being applied to the non-Yoknapatawpha fiction, and so Faulkner may have felt more at liberty to insert himself into these novels, either directly as man or indirectly as artist.

Partly for this reason, the non-Yoknapatawpha novels, strangely enough, seem in some respects more personal than their Yoknapatawpha counterparts. There are other reasons as well: for example, the apprenticeship novels present the young Faulkner, warts and all, uncertainly casting about for an appropriate mode of expression—for just that combination of material and narrative perspective, in fact, which he seems to have found at the moment he conceived of Yoknapatawpha County. And by virtue of the very fact that Yoknapatawpha forms such an imposing literary achievement, Faulkner might appear to be, and quite possibly may have felt, more vulnerable when venturing beyond its boundaries. Faulkner's choosing nevertheless to rove outside the secure, though mutable, perimeters of Yoknapatawpha after he had so thoroughly established and developed them testifies to his courage and dedication as a writer. The non-Yoknapatawpha novels thus demonstrate that Faulkner himself had avoided, or was in the process of avoiding, those same pitfalls into which the failed artist-figures in each book plunge headlong.

The status of the non-Yoknapatawpha novels as fables of creativity intensifies this special aura of personal investment. Taken as a group, they form Faulkner's most intense examination into the origin, meaning and function of art, his fictional casebook on writing, a workshop of 'uncharted' settings in which he explored ideas and techniques either rejected, modified, adopted, or maintained in the novels set in Yoknapatawpha. They may also be read as providing the reader of the canon with a 'traveller's guide' to the borders of Yoknapatawpha, not only demarcating those avenues of approach which are dead-ends but also indicating thoroughfares which lead directly to the heart of the fictional county and of the Faulknerian world.

Each of the non-Yoknapatawpha novels is radically experimental, and although some are more successful than others, when considered as a group they may be seen to provide a special kind of insight into the imaginative processes which shaped the canon. In fact, they provide for the reader that same distance and perspective in relation to Yoknapatawpha which they may well have furnished for Faulkner himself. Clearly an essential part of the canon—as much by virtue of as despite their deliberate separation from the central Yoknapatawpha texts—these five fables of creativity can properly be grouped together as works in which Faulkner, unconsciously at first, quite consciously later on, chose 'alien' settings for novels which would in some sense push outwards the perimeters of his art, his moral commitment, and his own sense of himself as man and as artist.

Notes

CHAPTER 1: INTRODUCTION

1. Yonce, '*Soldiers' Pay*: A Critical Study of William Faulkner's First Novel', Diss. University of South Carolina 1970; 'The Composition of *Soldiers' Pay*', *Mississippi Quarterly*, 33 (1980) 291–326; and 'Faulkner's "Atthis" and "Attis": Some Sources of Myth', *Mississippi Quarterly*, 23 (1970) 289–98; McHaney, *William Faulkner's 'The Wild Palms': A Study* (Jackson: University Press of Mississippi, 1975); Butterworth, *A Critical and Textual Study of Faulkner's 'A Fable'* (Ann Arbor: UMI, 1983).
2. Brooks, *William Faulkner: Toward Yoknapatawpha and Beyond* (New Haven: Yale University Press, 1978). Randolph E. Stein's 1965 dissertation, 'The World Outside Yoknapatawpha: A Study of Five Novels by William Faulkner', deals almost exclusively with the novels as separate texts, and his comments are now dated: many of his remarks, while perhaps of some value when the dissertation was written, have by the present time become critical commonplaces, while others—such as his reading of *Pylon* as an unrelenting attack on the spiritual wasteland of modern society and his view of the tall convict in *The Wild Palms* as a primitive hero—have since been discredited. Duane MacMillan's more recent dissertation, 'The Non-Yoknapatawpha Novels of William Faulkner: An Examination of *Soldiers' Pay, Mosquitoes, Pylon, The Wild Palms,* and *A Fable*' (1972), provides synopses of observations made by others on the non-Yoknapatawpha novels, and these in turn establish the foundation for his own detailed analyses. Although MacMillan occasionally develops worthwhile points, especially with regard to *A Fable,* his dissertation as a whole is hampered by his extreme reliance on Faulkner's Nobel Prize Address as a schema through which the entire canon must be interpreted. Indeed, although MacMillan takes issue with those commentators who read *A Fable* as a 'gloss' on the Nobel Prize Address, this is essentially his own position with each of the non-Yoknapatawpha novels. His statement that Faulkner's basic attitudes as expressed in Stockholm were present very early in his literary career, and consequently 'required little or no development or evolution' (297) during the subsequent forty years of that career, seems dubious in itself and dependent upon the assumption, evident throughout the dissertation, that Faulkner's novels tend more toward explication than exploration.

See Stein, 'The World Outside Yoknapatawpha: A Study of Five Novels by William Faulkner', Diss. Ohio University 1965, and MacMillan, 'The Non-Yoknapatawpha Novels of William Faulkner: An Examination of *Soldiers' Pay, Mosquitoes, Pylon, The Wild Palms,* and *A Fable*', Diss. University of Wisconsin 1972.

3. McHaney, 'Brooks on Faulkner: The End of the Long View', in *Review I*, eds James O. Hoge and James L. W. West, III (Charlottesville: University Press of Virginia, 1979) pp. 29–46.
4. See, for example, *Lion in the Garden: Interviews with William Faulkner 1926–62*, eds James B. Meriwether and Michael Millgate (New York: Random, 1968) p. 255.
5. For a valuable discussion of *Soldiers' Pay* and *Mosquitoes* as pre-Yoknapatawphan, apprenticeship fiction, see Martin Kreiswirth, *William Faulkner: The Making of a Novelist* (Athens, Georgia: University of Georgia Press, 1983).
6. See Joseph Blotner, *Faulkner: A Biography*. 2 vols. (New York: Random, 1974) pp. 508–10, 516–19.
7. See Michael Millgate, *The Achievement of William Faulkner* (London: Constable, 1966) pp. 138–41, and Brooks, pp. 395–405.

CHAPTER 2: SOLDIERS' PAY

1. Blotner, *Biography*, p. 397.
2. See Carvel Collins's introduction to *New Orleans Sketches*, augmented edition, ed. Carvel Collins (New York: Random, 1968) pp. xxi. Yonce notes that there is no manuscript evidence that this was the original title. See 'The Composition', p. 294.
3. For a more comprehensive synopsis of the pre-publication history of *Soldiers' Pay* see Blotner, *Biography*, pp. 397–515, and Yonce, 'The Composition'.
4. See Blotner, *Biography*, pp. 505–6, and *William Faulkner: The Critical Heritage*, ed. John Bassett (London: Routledge & Kegan Paul, 1975) pp. 52–62.
5. Vickery, *The Novels of William Faulkner* (Baton Rouge: Louisiana State University Press, 1964) pp. 1–7; Millgate, *The Achievement*, pp. 61–8 and 'Starting Out in the Twenties: Reflections on *Soldiers' Pay*', *Mosaic*, 7 (1973) 1–14; Brooks, *Toward Yoknapatawpha*, pp. 67–99 and 'Faulkner's First Novel', *Southern Review* NS 6 (1970) 1056–74; and Yonce, 'The Composition', 'Faulkner's "Atthis" ', and Diss.
6. *Soldiers' Pay* (New York: Boni & Liveright, 1926) p. 196. Subsequent references to *Soldiers' Pay* are from this edition and are noted parenthetically.
7. 'Sherwood Anderson' in *New Orleans Sketches*, p. 133.
8. 'Sherwood Anderson' in *New Orleans Sketches*, pp. 132–4.
9. *Dark Laughter* (New York: Boni & Liveright, 1925) p. 248.
10. Jones's yellow eyes anticipate Charlotte's 'yellow stare' in *The Wild Palms* and this correspondence serves in part to suggest their being aligned with each other as insufficient artist-figures.

11. Homer, *The Odyssey*, trans. Robert Fitzgerald (Garden City: Anchor Books, 1963) XVI, 211.
12. Stewart, *The Disguised Guest: Rank, Role, and Identity in the 'Odyssey'* (Lewisburg: Bucknell University Press, 1976) pp. 105, 109, 122–3.
13. *As I Lay Dying: The Corrected Text* (New York: Random, 1985) p. 162. André Bleikasten also notes the importance of Donald's need to regain his identity and briefly suggests that it may be an 'inverted emblem of Faulkner's own quest' regarding the author's relationship to his past. See Bleikasten, *The Most Splendid Failure: Faulkner's 'The Sound and the Fury'* (Bloomingdale: Indiana University Press, 1976) p. 20.
14. Yonce, Diss., pp. 18–19. Actually, Faulkner allowed one reference to Joe as 'Gilligan' to remain, which may have been, as Yonce suggests, an 'oversight' (Diss., p. 19).
15. *The Achievement*, p. 16.
16. Michael Grimwood, *Heart in Conflict: Faulkner's Struggles with Vocation* (Athens, Georgia: University of Georgia Press, 1987) p. 29.
17. 'Verse Old and Nascent: A Pilgrimage', in *William Faulkner: Early Prose and Poetry*, ed. Carvel Collins (Boston: Little, Brown, 1962) p. 115.
18. 'An Introduction for *The Sound and the Fury*', ed. James B. Meriwether, *Southern Review* NS 8 (1972) 708.
19. *Essays, Speeches & Public Letters*, ed. James B. Meriwether (New York: Random, 1965) p. 120.

CHAPTER 3: MOSQUITOES

1. *The Selected Letters of William Faulkner*, ed. Joseph Blotner (New York: Random, 1978) p. 40.
2. *Mosquitoes* (New York: Boni & Liveright, 1927) p. 186. Subsequent references to *Mosquitoes* are from this edition and are noted parenthetically.
3. See 'Out of Nazareth' in *New Orleans Sketches*, p. 53.
4. Brooks, 'Faulkner's *Mosquitoes*', *Georgia Review*, 31 (1977) 217.
5. Warren, 'Faulkner's "Portrait of the Artist" ', *Mississippi Quarterly*, 19 (1966) 121–31.
6. Frank Budgen, *James Joyce and the Making of 'Ulysses'* (New York: Smith & Haas, 1934) p. 60.
7. Richard Ellman, *James Joyce* (Oxford: Oxford University Press, 1959) p. 450.
8. Arnold, 'Freedom and Stasis in Faulkner's *Mosquitoes*', *Mississippi Quarterly*, 28 (1975) 289–90, and 'William Faulkner's *Mosquitoes*', Diss., University of South Carolina 1978, pp. xiv–xix, xxiii–xxiv.
9. See Blotner, *Biography*, p. 405, and Walter B. Rideout and James B. Meriwether, 'On the Collaboration of Faulkner and Anderson', *American Literature*, 35 (1963) 85–7.
10. Carvel Collins, 'Introduction' in *'Helen: A Courtship' and 'Mississippi*

Poems' (New Orleans and Oxford: Tulane University and Yoknapatawpha Press, 1981) p. 32.

11. For a discussion of other archetypal images in this scene, see David Williams, *Faulkner's Women: The Myth and the Muse* (Montreal and London: McGill-Queen's University Press, 1977) p. 36.
12. This is a general pattern rather than a precise schema. The entire 'Five O'Clock' episode, for instance, is devoted to Patricia and David.
13. *As I Lay Dying*, p. 160.
14. 'The Kid Learns' in *New Orleans Sketches*, p. 86.
15. Kenneth W. Hepburn in 'Faulkner's *Mosquitoes*: A Poetic Turning Point', *Twentieth Century Literature*, 17 (1971) 23, suggests that in section ten of the Epilogue Talliaferro attempts two 'artistic' acts.
16. Blotner, *Biography*, note-page 70.
17. While in New Orleans, interestingly enough, Faulkner, like Talliaferro, carried a walking stick and spoke with a vaguely British accent, and in the course of his career he twice used the first name 'Ernest' as a pseudonym: once, in 1925, in a facetious letter to H. L. Mencken urging him to publish a poem by one William Faulkner and again, much later, when he published 'Afternoon of a Cow' under the name of his 'amanuensis', Ernest V. Trueblood. See Blotner, *Biography*, p. 480, and *Uncollected Stories of William Faulkner*, ed. Joseph Blotner (New York: Random, 1979) p. 703. See also Grimwood, p. 34, who sees a further connection in the fact that just as Faulkner had altered the spelling of his family name from 'Falkner', so does Talliaferro change his name from 'Tarver'.
18. See also Max Putzel, *Genius of Place: William Faulkner's Triumphant Beginnings* (Baton Rouge: Louisiana State University Press, 1985) pp. 91–5.
19. Blotner, *Biography*, p. 502.
20. 'Carcassonne', in *The Collected Stories of William Faulkner* (New York: Random, 1977) p. 899.
21. *The Wild Palms* (New York: Random, 1939) p. 324.
22. *The Collected Poems of Dylan Thomas* (New York: New Directions, 1971) p. 47.

CHAPTER 4: PYLON

1. Ernest Hemingway, 'On Being Shot Again: A Gulf Stream Letter', reprinted in *By-Line: Ernest Hemingway Selected Articles and Dispatches of Four Decades*, ed. William White (New York: Scribners, 1967) p. 200.
2. *Ernest Hemingway: Selected Letters 1917–1961*, ed. Carlos Baker (New York: Granada, 1981) p. 864; see also p. 863.
3. *The Fourteenth Chronicle: Letters and Diaries of John Dos Passos*, ed. Townsend Ludington (Boston: Gambit, 1973) p. 636.
4. *Pylon* (New York: Smith & Haas, 1935) p. 149. Subsequent references to *Pylon* are from this edition and are noted parenthetically.

5. In fact, one contemporary reviewer did make this connection. See T. S. Mathews's otherwise rather pointless parody of *Pylon* in *The Critical Heritage*, pp. 185–7. M. Thomas Inge investigates the possible influence of comic strips upon Faulkner's early drawings. He mentions *Bringing Up Father* specifically, although not with reference to *Pylon*. See 'Faulkner Reads the Funny Papers', in *Faulkner and Humor: Faulkner and Yoknapatawpha, 1984*, eds Doreen Fowler and Ann J. Abadie (Jackson: University of Mississippi Press, 1986) pp. 153–90.
6. For commentary on this phenomenon, see Ron Goulart, *The Adventurous Decade: Comic Strips in the Thirties* (New Rochelle: Arlington House, 1975) pp. 101–22. For remarks on *Bringing Up Father*, see Colton Waugh, *The Comics* (New York: Macmillan, 1947) p. 47.
7. See also Millgate, *The Achievement*, p. 145.
8. John Dos Passos, *Three Plays: 'The Garbage Man', 'Airways, Inc.', 'Fortune Heights'* (New York: Harcourt, Brace, 1934) p. 155.
9. John Dos Passos, *Manhattan Transfer* (New York: Harper, 1925) p. 299.
10. *Lion in the Garden*, p. 132.
11. At the University of Virginia, Faulkner described barnstormers as a 'fantastic and bizarre phenomenon on the face of a contemporary scene' and continued: 'there was really no place for them in the culture, in the economy, yet they were there . . . . [They] wanted just enough money to live, to get to the next place to race again. Something frenetic and in a way almost immoral about it. That they were outside the range of God, not only of respectability, of love, but of God too. That they had escaped the compulsion of accepting a past and a future, that they were—they had no past. They were as ephemeral as the butterfly that's born this morning with no stomach and will be gone tomorrow'. *Faulkner in the University: Class Conferences at the University of Virginia 1957–1958*, eds Frederick L. Gwynn and Joseph L. Blotner (New York: Vintage, 1965) p. 36.
12. *Lion in the Garden*, p. 252.
13. *Lion in the Garden*, p. 267.
14. Review of *Test Pilot*, in *Essays*, p. 189. See also 'The Uncut Text of Faulkner's Review of *Test Pilot*', ed. James B. Meriwether, *Mississippi Quarterly*, 33 (1980) 385–9.
15. *Lion in the Garden*, pp. 131–2.
16. *Letters*, 86–7.
17. T. S. Eliot, *The Complete Poems and Plays* (New York: Harcourt, Brace, 1952) p. 6.
18. *The Achievement*, p. 145.
19. See *The Oxford Dictionary of Saints* (Oxford: Clarendon, 1978) p. 79.
20. *Go Down, Moses and Other Stories* (New York: Random, 1942), p. 154.
21. *Faulkner in the University*, p. 36.
22. For an analysis of the ways in which Faulkner alters or manipulates traditional New Orleans Mardi Gras festivities to reinforce the wasteland atmosphere of New Valois in *Pylon*, see Susie Paul John-

son, '*Pylon*: Faulkner's Waste Land', *Mississippi Quarterly*, 38 (1985) 287–94.

23. That Laverne's leaving of Jackie with Dr Shumann should generate some sympathy for her becomes apparent when one compares her doing so with Charlotte Rittenmeyer's abandoning her children in *The Wild Palms*. Whereas Laverne is impelled by her interest in Jackie's welfare, Charlotte's motives are predominantly selfish. It is congruent with Laverne's life-affirming attitude that she is pregnant at the conclusion of *Pylon*; it is equally appropriate that Charlotte's life-denying tendencies should become manifest in her death as a result of the botched abortion in *The Wild Palms*.
24. Eliot, *Complete Poems*, p. 21.
25. See *Faulkner in the University*, pp. 273–4.
26. Blotner, *Biography*, pp. 865–6, 870; and Millgate, *The Achievement*, pp. 150–1.
27. The reporter's reference to the Florentine tragedy may contain an allusion to the love-triangle in 'The Novel of the Curious Impertinent' in *Don Quixote*. Another possible source is Oscar Wilde's fragmentary play, *A Florentine Tragedy*, which was available in the 1905 *Collected Works* and subsequent editions.
28. *Faulkner in the University*, p. 39.

CHAPTER 5: THE WILD PALMS

1. See *Critical Heritage*, pp. 230–50.
2. Grimwood, p. 109.
3. McHaney, *A Study*, p. 38. The changing of the date from 1927 to 1937 also served to render the action in 'Wild Palms' more nearly contemporaneous with the times of the novel's composition and publication. Grimwood notes that 'Wild Palms' is topical as well in its relation to the 'ambulatory novels' which proliferated during the Depression, often featuring a young couple travelling around the country 'in search of America'. See Grimwood, p. 127.
4. *Letters*, p. 338.
5. *The Wild Palms* (New York: Random, 1939) p. 52. Subsequent references to *The Wild Palms* are from this edition and are noted parenthetically.
6. McHaney, *A Study*, p. 156.
7. See *Faulkner in the University*, pp. 243–4; and Millgate, 'Faulkner's Masters', *Tulane Studies in English*, 23 (1978) 143–55. Pamela Rhodes and Richard Godden have located possible influences on 'Wild Palms' in two works roughly contemporaneous with it: James M. Cain's *The Postman Always Rings Twice* (1934) and Horace McCoy's *They Shoot Horses, Don't They?* (1935). See Rhodes and Godden, '*The Wild Palms*: Degraded Culture, Devalued Texts' in *Intertextuality in Faulkner*, eds Michel Gresset and Noel Polk (Jackson: University Press of Mississippi, 1985) pp. 87–92.
8. See, for example, *Lion in the Garden*, p. 250.

9. See, for example, *Lion in the Garden*, pp. 247–8.
10. Samuel Beckett, *Proust* (New York: Grove, 1957) p. 10.
11. See *Lion in the Garden*, p. 240.
12. McHaney, *A Study*, p. xvii.
13. See also McHaney, *A Study*, p. 72.
14. The negative effects of Charlotte's manipulation of Harry may be suggested by the fact that her distorted figure of Cyrano holds 'a piece of cheese in one hand and a check book in the other' (91); when Harry first arrives at the party at which he meets Charlotte, Flint introduces him as 'Doctor Wilbourne' and states: 'Watch him. He's got a pad of blank checks in his pocket and a scalpel in his sleeve' (37).
15. *Faulkner in the University*, pp. 175, 183.
16. Anderson, *The Triumph of the Egg* (New York: Huebsch, 1921) p. 170.
17. For one of many examples, see *Faulkner in the University*, p. 19.
18. This narrative strategy resembles that involving Laverne and Jackie at Dr Shumann's home in *Pylon* in which it is clearly Faulkner, rather than the reporter, who relates the episode. Faulkner employs a similar technique in *A Fable*, but for a very different purpose. In that work, Sutterfield nominally provides the runner with the detailed story of the horsethief episode; nevertheless, the account is in the third person, includes events which the preacher could not have witnessed, and displays a level of sophistication in expression beyond that which could reasonably be attributed to him. In *A Fable*, however, Faulkner seems to be emphasizing Sutterfield's positive potential as an interpreter of the verities rather than, as with the reporter in *Pylon* and the convict in *The Wild Palms*, indicating inadequacies in that same role.
19. *Lion in the Garden*, p. 72.
20. Faulkner may well have had Anderson particularly in mind while writing *The Wild Palms*, having met with the older writer several times in New York City in 1937 when the novel was in its early stages of development. See Blotner, *Biography*, pp. 974–5.
21. *Essays*, p. 10.
22. A response related both to the impact of the Cajun's hides on the tall convict and to the influence of Anderson's way of life on Faulkner occurs in 'Wild Palms' when Harry stands mesmerized before the painting at the party where he meets Charlotte: 'Wilbourne stood before the paintings in complete absorption. . . . It was in a bemusement without heat or envy at a condition which could supply a man with the obvious leisure and means to spend his days painting such as this and his evenings playing the piano and feeding liquor to people whom he ignored'. (38) Interestingly enough, Harry not only tries to paint in Wisconsin but also describes himself to the doctor in the first chapter as a painter. See also Grimwood, p. 115, and Rhodes and Godden, pp. 106–7.
23. See Blotner, *Biography*, p. 405, and Rideout and Meriwether, pp. 85–7.

24. A Note on 'Sherwood Anderson' in *Essays*, p. 8.
25. Pamela Rhodes and Richard Godden associate the convict's 'probing for the life' of the alligators with Harry's performing the abortions in 'Wild Palms'. See Rhodes and Godden, p. 107.
26. Given the implicit correspondence between the Cajun and Sherwood Anderson, it is even possible to detect a correlation between the Cajun's administering the sunburn salve to the tall convict and Anderson's visiting Faulkner at the Algonquin to comfort him after he had burned his back. For details of Anderson's visit, see Blotner, *Biography*, p. 975.
27. In the related episode involving the convict's reaction to whiskey aboard the steamboat, Faulkner may well have been poking fun at the distorted contemporary view of himself as a bucolic misfit who had visions under the influence of alcohol.
28. See also Arnold, Diss., p. 128.
29. McHaney, 'William Faulkner's *The Wild Palms*', Diss. University of South Carolina 1979, p. 293. Had the punctuation in the typescript been followed, the lack of closure in this final sentence of the novel would produce much the same effect as that achieved by the similar strategy in the conclusion of *Pylon*, Faulkner once again emphasising the necessity of the reader's completing the work after having read the last page.
30. See McHaney, *A Study*, p. 29.
31. *Go Down, Moses*, p. 363.
32. Soren Kierkegaard, 'The Ancient Tragical Motif as Reflected in the Modern' in *Tragedy: Vision and Form*, ed. Robert W. Corrigan (San Francisco: Chandler, 1965) pp. 455–6.
33. *Faulkner in the University*, p. 51.
34. See McHaney, *A Study*, p. xiv.
35. *Letters*, p. 106.
36. See also Rhodes and Godden, p. 97. Charlotte's affinities with Helen Baird and Meta Carpenter may be pertinent in that in 'Wild Palms' Faulkner is himself perhaps keeping alive the memory of a love that he, like Harry, had lost, although in a much different manner and under very different circumstances.
37. *Letters*, p. 228.
38. See, for example, *Lion in the Garden*, p. 255.
39. While Charlotte does not achieve the death by water which she advocates, she does, like Quentin, die in early June. For the approximate date of her death, see McHaney, *A Study*, p. 200.
40. In this context, Flint's mention of the 'Saint Charles' hotel with reference to Harry and Charlotte's initial assignation (44) assumes additional significance.
41. *The Portable Faulkner*, ed. Malcolm Cowley (New York: Viking, 1946) p. 743.
42. *The Sound and the Fury*: *The Corrected Text* (New York: Random, 1984) p. 199.
43. *The Portable Faulkner*, p. 744.
44. For less positive formulations of Harry's refusal to commit suicide

and of his experience as a whole after being incarcerated, see Rhodes and Godden, pp. 99–100, and Francois Pitavy 'Forgetting Jerusalem: An Ironical Chart for *The Wild Palms*' in *Intertextuality in Faulkner*, eds Michel Gresset and Noel Polk (Jackson: University Press of Mississippi, 1985) pp. 114–27.

45. *The Sound and the Fury*, p. 197, Faulkner's italics.
46. *Go Down, Moses*, pp. 130–1.
47. Bleikasten, *The Most Splendid Failure*, p. 93.
48. *The Sound and the Fury*, p. 198.
49. At the University of Virginia, Faulkner remarked on Quentin's narration, saying 'Quentin is a dying man, he is already out of life, and those things that were important in life don't mean anything to him any more'. *Faulkner in the University*, p. 18.

CHAPTER 6: A FABLE

1. *Letters*, p. 262.
2. See Blotner, *Biography*, pp. 1117–526.
3. *Letters*, p. 179.
4. Cowley, *The Faulkner-Cowley File: Letters and Memories 1944–1962* (New York: Viking, 1966) p. 105. Although Faulkner referred to the work as 'a fable' almost from its inception, Blotner dates the actual choice of the title much later than does Cowley. See Blotner, *Biography*, p. 1470.
5. Butterworth, p. 2.
6. *Letters*, p. 201.
7. *Letters*, pp. 191 and 233.
8. *Letters*, p. 188.
9. *Letters*, p. 352.
10. Blotner, *Biography*, p. 1506.
11. For a detailed study of early reviews and articles, see Schendler, 'William Faulkner's *A Fable*', Diss. Northwestern University 1956, pp. 1–39. See also Straumann, 'An American Interpretation of Existence: Faulkner's *A Fable*', in *William Faulkner: Three Decades of Criticism*, eds Frederick J. Hoffman and Olga W. Vickery (Lansing: Michigan State University Press, 1960) pp. 349–72.
12. *A Fable* (New York: Random, 1954) p. 161. Subsequent references to *A Fable* are from this edition and are noted parenthetically.
13. *Lion in the Garden*, p. 247.
14. See also Butterworth, pp. 21–5.
15. Millgate, 'Faulkner on the Literature of the First World War', *Mississippi Quarterly*, 26 (1973) 392. It is also possible that Faulkner may have chosen World War I as a setting in order to respond to Hemingway's use of that same setting in *A Farewell to Arms*, the work which Faulkner had more specifically addressed in *The Wild Palms*.
16. Faulkner's concern during the writing of *A Fable* with the interaction between reader and text seems to be obliquely indicated by his intention at one point during the concurrent composition of *Intruder*

in the Dust to have Gavin Stevens remark upon a book he had read by a Southern writer, one of whose principal characters was Shreve McCannon. See Blotner, *Biography*, note-page 169.

17. In his profession as a couturier, in his martial inexperience, and in his fundamental integrity, honesty and courage, Gragnon's aide bears a noteworthy resemblance to Francis Feeble, the 'woman's tailor' whom Falstaff recruits as a soldier in Shakespeare's *2 Henry IV*, III, ii. The aide's civilian occupation also recalls that of Talliaferro in *Mosquitoes*.
18. That much of *Gil Blas* is devoted to the matter of writing provides another feature which may have appealed to Faulkner. Gil periodically associates with writers, and he himself becomes not only an author of sorts but also a critic and, unfortunately for his position in life, an honest one. It is also possible that Faulkner's description of the physical appearance of the runner after the barrage was influenced by the description of Don Hannibal in *Gil Blas*, who is similarly maimed and disfigured.
19. Butterworth, p. 39.
20. In Joseph Conrad's *Lord Jim*, Jim's occupation as a 'runner' for Blake and Egstrom while he attempts to shirk responsiblity for the Patna incident carries much the same impact as does the runner's military designation in *A Fable*.
21. Although Faulkner undoubtedly had other contexts in mind in the use of this quotation, the runner must perforce be making reference to *The Jew of Malta*. For a discussion of the multiple layers of this allusion in *A Fable*, see Phyllis Bartlett, 'Other Countries, Other Wenches' *Modern Fiction Studies*, 3 (1958) 348–9, and Richard P. Adams, *Faulkner: Myth and Motion* (Princeton: Princeton University Press, 1968) p. 11.
22. See also Kathryn Chittick, ' "Telling It Again and Again" ': *Notes on a Horsethief*', *Mississippi Quarterly*, 32 (1979) 426, 428; and Butterworth, pp. 54–5.
23. Chittick, p. 426.
24. *Faulkner in the University*, p. 62.
25. *Lion in the Garden*, p. 247.
26. *Lion in the Garden*, p. 255.
27. *Faulkner in the University*, p. 62.
28. *Essays*, pp. 137–8.
29. *William Faulkner Manuscripts 20: 'A Fable'*. Introduced and arranged by Michael Millgate, I (New York and London: Garland, 1986) pp. xiii–xiv.
30. *The Complete Poetry and Prose of William Blake*, ed. David V. Erdman (Berkeley: University of California Press, 1982) p. 35.
31. Millgate, *The Achievement*, p. 228.
32. *Letters*, p. 314. William Rossky asserts that *The Reivers* shares affinities with *The Tempest*; see his 'Faulkner's *Tempest*' in *William Faulkner: Four Decades of Criticism*, ed. Linda Welshimer Wagner (Lansing: Michigan State University Press, 1973) pp. 358–69.

CHAPTER 7: CONCLUSION

1. While some less positive non-Yoknapatawphan figures also travel substantially, Faulkner implies that their severely limited perspectives prevent them from benefitting from the experience.
2. For an analysis of the use of philosophic sources in *The Wild Palms*, for example, see McHaney, *A Study*, pp. xvii–xix, 31, and *passim*.
3. *A Faulkner Miscellany*, ed. James B. Meriwether (Jackson: University Press of Mississippi, 1974) pp. 162–3.
4. *Lion in the Garden*, p. 238.

Index